ABOUT THE AUTHOR

Adrian Bradbury was born and raised in Manchester. He spent a happy childhood playing football, cricket, rugby, hide-and-seek, knock-a-door-run and anything else that would get him out of doing any work.

After a spell as a secondary school PE teacher he ran away to work overseas. This gave him chance to study lesser-known local sports such as Haddock Hurling (Sweden), All-in Camel Mud Wrestling (Oman), Cheese Jumping (France), Indoor Sausage Counting (Germany) and the famously vicious Motorised Mangoball (Indonesia).

During his travels he also worked undercover for Military Intelligence (or lack of, in his case). In 1987 he successfully foiled an Eskimo plot to move the North Pole further to the left. Captured behind enemy lines, he was ruthlessly tortured with dried mackerel before making a daring escape across the ice on the back of a sympathetic walrus called Toby (*translation of Eskimo name 'Aaaaaruffn'*). He quit the secret service in disgust in 1994 when, after dramatically saving the Emperor of Mongolia from cheesecake poisoning, he was rewarded with only a month's supply of frozen buffalo fat, a broken Casio watch and 5000 Mongolian Quarps (equal to 6.4p).

Since returning to England he has worked in Middle and Primary schools, as both teacher and ~~Chief Torturer~~ Deputy Head.

He lives in Torquay with his world-famous collection of electrical plugs and his pet stick insect, Pritt. *

---

* *Not all of these details may be entirely accurate.*

This book is dedicated to all the childen I've ever taught
who've made me laugh, especially those at
St Marychurch and Sherwell Valley Primary Schools, Torquay.
May your laughs get ever louder!

Special thanks to:

Debbie and Richard Hancox
For all their freely given time and help

Julia Hill
for her brilliant artwork and wacky sense of humour!

Darren James, Iain Williamson, John Cornforth and Leroy Rosenior
For their expert help and opinions

Ian Shapland
For his superb cartoons

Colin Bratcher and Paul Levie
For allowing me to use their terrific photos (for free!)

Mark and Rob at Short Run Press
For their patient guidance of a typesetting dunce

ID
Torquay United FC
2005~2006

A ~~Y~~ ^{dramatic} YEAR IN THE LIFE OF THE GULLS!!

by Adrian Bradbury

Illustrated by Julia Hill and Ian Shapland

Bobby Dazzler Publishing Ltd

Published in 2006 by Bobby Dazzler Publishing Ltd

Copyright © Bobby Dazzler Publishing Ltd,
24 Lisburne Place
Torquay

All rights reserved

Photos reproduced by kind permission of:
Colin Bratcher
Paul Levie
Herald Express newspapers.

ISBN   0-9553511-0-3
978-0-9553511-0-5

Printed in UK by Short Run Press Ltd, Exeter

Contents

Introduction 6

August 10

Down Memory Lane 18

Pretty Easy Challenges..27

September 34

Who Am I??? (1) 40

October 41

Training 46

Still Pretty Easy Challenges..53

November 59

Who Am I??? (2) 64

December 65

The Fizzy O!..72

January 79

Bit 'arder Challenges 88

February..95

March 102

Nicknames/Grounds Quiz 108

The Ref! 109

April 119

Dead 'ard Challenges 130

May..138

Alphabet Quiz 148

Extras..149

Answers 155

5

Introduction

READ THIS FIRST!

Before you start on this book I need to let you in on a secret. You're not going to like this, but if we're going to get on together we need to be honest with each other right from the word go ....

        I used to be a teacher.

NO! DO **NOT** PUT THIS BOOK BACK ON THE SHELF!

Sorry, I didn't mean to shout at you. It's the teacher in me, it comes to the surface occasionally. Don't worry, I am having therapy but it's a long slow process. Actually, when I say I used to be a teacher, I'm not really telling the whole story. It's a bit worse than that ......

        I used to be a Deputy Head.

OI!! **DON'T YOU DARE** THROW THE BOOK IN THE BIN! SOMEONE PAID FIVE QUID FOR THAT! GET IT OUT THIS MINUTE!

        I'LL TELL YOUR MUM ....

There, that's better. Now, let's both calm down shall we? What I was trying to get across was that I'm now pretty much cured. I used to be the type who'd take great delight in seeing children suffer, the type who'd smile contentedly as he told you how much trouble you were in. Know the sort? Well I'm glad to say I've seen the light. Ok, there is the odd urge to pull a small child's hair now and again, but that usually passes before I manage to get a really tight grip on it, and I can honestly say that I can count on the fingers of one hand the number of children that I've made cry in the last ...... 24 hours.

No, I've realised that schools aren't always the best places to learn things. You don't really need to sit in a classroom to learn, and learning doesn't have to be serious. When I set out writing this book I had three things in mind:

1. To help you find out more about what goes on in your favourite football club, and to show you what a smashing little club Torquay United is.

2. To give you a chance to show how clever you are by taking on some of the football challenges I've set you. I've grouped them in four sections through the book: Pretty Easy, Still Pretty Easy, Bit 'arder and Dead 'ard. Feel free to have a go at any or all of them. Find your own level. And promise me one thing: the words "It's too hard!" or "Do I have to?" won't pass your lips. Just like in football, the tougher the situation, the more effort you need to put in!

I've also bunged in some quizzes to stretch your ickle brain cells. If you don't know an answer you might try the internet if you have access. If not, you'll need a dictionary, atlas or ~~encyclopiar enciclopeed ensyklo~~ reference book. Or you might just ask a friend, teacher (yeh, right! As if *they'd* know) or parent. A word of warning here: DO NOT GIVE IN TO BLACKMAIL!!! If they try the old trick of *"I'll tell you the answer if you do the washing up!"* treat that pathetic offer with the scorn it deserves and go and ask someone cleverer instead.

3. To give you a laugh. I've tried to write the book so that anyone from 8 to 18 can enjoy it. If some of the language is a bit difficult for you younger ones then I'm sorry, but it's never easy trying to keep everybody happy. Just don't give up - it'll help to develop your reading skills.

So please read this book with a smile on your face. After all you've got reasons to be cheerful – your team almost went out of the Football League last season. They were just about dead and buried as far as league football was concerned, but by a miracle they live to fight again another day.

And after you've read the book, please pester your dad to take you along to Plainmoor to watch a game. Then, when you love it so much, pester him to take you to the next match too. A good tip for this is to have a word with your mum, cos it's a safe bet that she'll be more than happy to get both of you out of the house on a Saturday afternoon so she can have a bit of peace and quiet.

We've seen from experience that the more fans there are at the game, the better the atmosphere and the better the team plays. Torquay United needs you, the league needs great little clubs like Torquay United, Torquay needs Torquay United, and so do we! *

ENJOY!

* Sorry if that last bit's confusing, but I had a bet that I could get the word 'Torquay' into a sentence four times. I'm now ten quid richer!

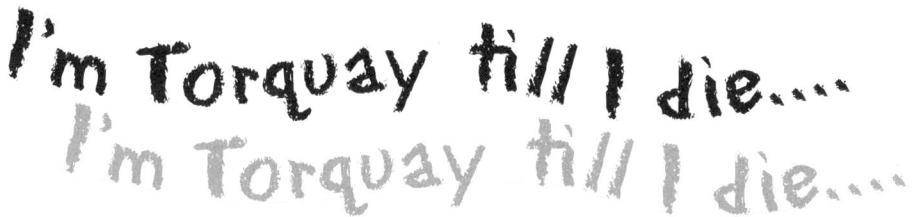

You might sing it on the terraces, but IS IT TRUE???

Before you can read on, I'm afraid you're going to have to take my introductory test! *(answers page 155)*

1.	What's the name of United's ground?
2.	Roughly how many fans does the stadium hold? 　　a) 2,000　　b) 6,000　　c) 20,000　　d) 50,000
3.	How much does it cost for a child to get in for a league match?
4.	What two colours make up United's home kit?
5.	Last season United had 3 managers. Can you name them all?
6.	Which royal runs the TUFC Football In The Community scheme?
7.	Who did United play on the dramatic final day of last season?
8.	What's United's nickname?
9.	What's the mascot called?
10.	What are the first names of these players? 　　a) Taylor　　b) Angus　　c) Garner　　d) Thorpe

Score 10:	You really *are* Torquay till you die!
Score 7-9:	Torquay till you're a bit wrinkly!
Score 4-6:	Torquay till you switch to Chelsea or Man Utd!
Score 0-3:	Torquay till bed time tonight!

August

August. Aaahhh! Just the mention of the word brings a dreamy smile of contentment to the face.

The Summer holidays. Mmmmmm…….. How many Ms does it take to express the sheer ecstacy of waking up knowing you don't have to go to school? Let's try 12:

Mmmmmmmmmmmm!!!

I'm not sure that's enough, though I suppose it depends on who you are. If you're one of those geeks who loves nothing better than to get their teeth into some tricky maths problem, or write a fascinating report on Why Fish Don't Have Toes (yes, believe me, there *are* people out there who are turned on by such things!), then one or two might be enough. If you're a normal child, however, it could be anything between 10 and 371. I'd show you what that looks like, only I don't want to use up all my Ms in case I need them later in the book.

Now if it was a question of how long you might lie in bed instead of getting up for school, it would be no problem. You could have a little snoozette - zzzzzz ………………

.... or you can stay in bed till tea time:

ZZZZZZZZZZZZZZZZZZZZZZZZZZZZZZZZZZZZZZZZZZZZZZZZZZZZZZZZZZZZZZZZZZZZZZZZZZZZZZZZZZZ

August

I can spare you as many Zs as you need, cos I probably won't need them later on. In fact, that can be your first challenge:

How many famous footballers or clubs can you think of that have a Z in their name???

If you can find 5 or more, send them in an E-mail to this address:

bobby_dazzler@fsmail.net

Sorry, where was I? Asleep? Possibly. School? Ahem, please don't mention that word. August? That's it, August ......

Six sun-filled, fun-filled weeks with no school. Absolute, undiluted bliss! Staying in bed till lunchtime. Munching toast and jam while you watch daytime TV. Going down the beach with your mates. In the park being Freddy Flintoff, scoring a brilliant century against those Aussies to win

August

the Ashes, then Wayne Rooney in your back garden, cracking the sudden-death penalty into the top corner (or next door's kitchen window) to win the 2010 World Cup, punching the air in triumph and then raising your arms and turning to acknowledge the screams of your adoring .... parents!!?? (aaaagh!!), nagging at you yet again about how you keep putting off those jobs they've asked you at least a thousand times to do. I expect you know the script off by heart by now - "When are you going to tidy that pig sty of a bedroom? That bike won't clean itself you know! Turn The Simpsons off (doh!), get off your lazy backside and go and give your dad a hand clearing out the garage! If that car's not washed by 3 o'clock you can kiss goodbye to your spends for this week!" etc etc, bla bla bla. Don't they realise you're on holiday??? I mean, derrrr!

Putting aside the minor irritation of parents, there's another major plus to August - the start of a new football season. The rich promise of success for your club, and all those questions waiting to be answered:

1. Will mum buy me the new away kit, even though I never quite got round to tidying my room?

2. Will dad for once set off a bit earlier so we can park closer than two miles from the ground and get to kick off without needing emergency oxygen or blister cream?

3. Shall I have red or brown sauce on my half-time chips? Hm, tricky one that.

Although Leroy Rosenior probably wasn't asking himself exactly those questions (he'd already got the kit and he was obviously far too busy to eat chips at half-time), he would no doubt have been looking forward to the new season with the same tingle of excitement as you.

Ok, during the close season he'd lost the services of two key players. Midfield playmaker Alex Russell wanted Division 1 football and signed for Bristol City, while previous season's top scorer Adebayo Akinfenwa couldn't resist the temptation to play alongside Lee Trundle at Swansea City, again in Division 1. Even so, you might expect that having just been relegated from a higher division, a team should be able to cope comfortably with the challenge of lower league football. Shouldn't they?

In fact this usually doesn't turn out to be the case. Just look at the Premiership - relegated teams very often find themselves struggling in the bottom half of the Coca Cola Championship the next season. So, like all good managers, Leroy spent his summer doing all he could to put together a squad which would push for promotion straight back up to Division 1.

This wasn't an easy task. United can't afford to pay as much as some of their rivals, while players themselves may look upon Torquay as a bit out of the way, isolated from the country's main areas of football action. They may also need a little extra persuasion to sign for a club that has just been relegated.

If that's the case, Leroy must have a silver tongue, because he managed to strengthen the squad by attracting not one or two, but eleven new players to Plainmoor for the start of the season!

Darren Garner	-	from loan to full contract
Matt Villis	-	from loan to full contract
Alan Connell	-	from Bournemouth
Matt Hewlett	-	from Swindon Town
Alex Lawless	-	from Fulham
James Sharp	-	from Brechin City
Liam Coleman	-	from Colchester City
James Bittner	-	from Exeter City
Morike Sako	-	from somewhere in France
Mamadou Sow	-	from somewhere in France
Carl Priso	-	from somewhere in France

August

Sorry to be a bit vague about the origins of the French trio, but Leroy was playing his cards close to his chest on that one.

All in all then we could look forward to a flying start to the season, with the Gulls up there challenging for the top spot right from the off. With the season starting early due to the need for a break before the World Cup in June, United had six league games to play in August - a heavy schedule. A possible 18 points. Two or three wins would see us comfortably mid-table by the end of the month. Three or four wins and a draw would probably put us straight into the play-off positions, which we could use as a platform to push on from in our promotion quest.

....

Well, it didn't quite work out that way.

United had much the better of a disappointing 0-0 draw with Notts County on the opening day, but despite outplaying their visitors the ball just wouldn't go in the net. Andy Marriott gave a hint of things to come when he saved brilliantly at the death to rescue a point, while a red card for Tony Bedeau resulted in a one-match ban. This stuttering start to the season turned into a rather poor start and then a disastrous start, as three defeats followed in the next ten days. If the 0-1 loss at Oxford United could be seen as a little unlucky, the performance in the 0-3 defeat at Mansfield on a difficult wet surface was best summed up by Leroy's after-match comment: "Utter rubbish!" For the first time in the season United found themselves bottom of the league.

So far our goal-scoring record in three matches was ..... none. Not a sausage. If you only followed the club by listening to the scores on the radio, you could be forgiven for thinking the club was called Torquay United Nil. Clearly something had to be put right. It looked like a magic wand had been waved when cool finishes from Constantine and Hewlett saw us 2-0 up against Bristol Rovers with less than quarter of an hour to play. At last, the win to get our season going. Or so we thought. Somehow, in one of those mad endings that we've come to expect from the Gulls (is there an angel with a wicked sense of humour up there watching over us???) we managed to let in three late goals. When the equaliser went in after 87 minutes you kind of knew it wouldn't stop there, that'd be too simple - there had to be one final twist. Maybe a swarm of giant killer bees would descend on Plainmoor, or an alien spaceship would hover over the ground, suck up all the players and erase the memories of all the fans with a gamma ray gun. Of course it was worse than both of those - an injury time winner for Bristol.

At least the club could take some heart from the fact that they'd at last managed to find the net, which was more than could be said on the Monday morning when the Plainmoor gates were opened - thieves had sneaked in during the night and nicked one of the goalnets! Know how much it costs for those bits of string to be replaced? £300! That's equal to 750 packets of Cheese and Onion crisps, 650 Mars bars or about three zillion Gummi Bears! (ok, I'm guessing at that last one)

Man City manager Stuart Pearce gets in to work one morning to find a very upset caretaker.
Caretaker: Bad news boss, burglars broke into the ground during the night.
Pearce: Oh no! What about all the cups?
Caretaker: It's all right boss, they didn't get as far as the kitchen.

Maybe the Carling Cup game against Bournemouth would provide a break from the league misery and give us something to cheer about. Alas, after a decent display Constantine was unable to convert the best chance of the match in the last minute of extra time, and we went down 4-3 on penalties. Surely things could only get better .....

Well, I suppose an away draw at Peterborough was a step in the right direction, even though again we failed to hit the net. At least it took us off the bottom of the table......for two days! Losing to an injury time goal at home to Chester dumped us back down there again. The crowd were

Joke!

understandably beginning to get restless. At the last full-time whistle of the month Andy Marriott's heroics saw him get a standing ovation from the Plainmoor faithful, while the rest of the team were booed off the pitch!

So, after such high hopes at 3 o'clock on August 3rd, by 5 o'clock on August 29th Torquay were bottom of the Football League, out of the Carling Cup, and had as many points as they had goals ..... 2!

> **August Quotes:**
>
> *"Utter rubbish! A disgrace!"*
> **Leroy rips into the team after the 3-0 defeat at Mansfield.**
>
> *"I felt like quitting!"*
> **Chairman Mike Bateson, after witnessing the disgraceful scenes of violence that saw 7 Bristol Rovers fans arrested and 30 more ejected from Plainmoor.**

August Stats

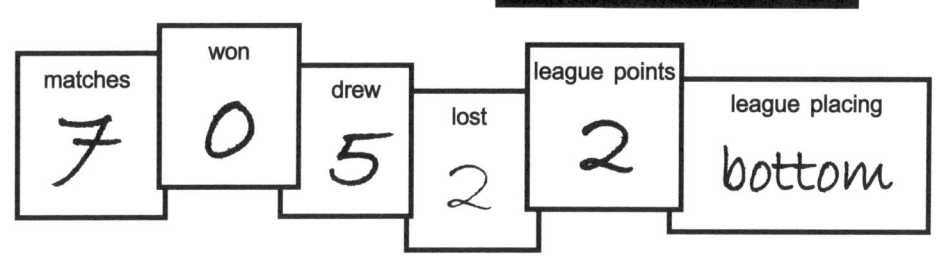

matches	7
won	0
drew	5
lost	2
league points	2
league placing	bottom

goals scored	scorers:	goals conceded
2	Constantine, Hewlett	8

players used	19
average match time in possession of ball	47%

yellow cards	red cards
10	1

fouls	by United	by opponents
	92	100

goal attempts	by United	by opponents
	63	115

total attendance	total miles travelled
22,793	1,374

Ave: 3,256

Table at end of August

	P	W	D	L	F	A	GD	Pts
Notts County	6	4	2	0	9	4	5	14
Darlington	6	3	2	1	10	7	3	11
Wycombe W.	6	2	4	0	10	5	5	10
Rochdale	6	3	1	2	11	7	4	10
Cheltenham	6	2	4	0	9	5	4	10
Grimsby Town	5	3	1	1	6	3	3	10
Barnet	6	3	1	2	8	7	1	10
Leyton Orient	6	3	1	2	7	8	-1	10
Chester City	5	2	3	0	9	7	2	9
Northampton	6	2	3	1	7	6	1	9
Wrexham	6	2	2	2	7	5	2	8
Peterborough	6	2	2	2	6	5	1	8
Carlisle United	6	2	2	2	4	5	-1	8
Lincoln City	6	1	4	1	7	7	0	7
Oxford United	5	1	3	1	5	5	0	6
Rushden / D.	5	1	3	1	4	5	-1	6
Shrewsbury	6	1	3	1	4	6	-2	6
Mansfield T.	6	1	2	3	9	10	-1	5
Stockport C.	6	0	5	1	7	9	-2	5
Bristol Rovers	5	1	1	3	7	10	-3	4
Macclesfield	5	1	1	3	5	8	-3	4
Bury	6	1	1	4	6	11	-5	4
Boston United	6	0	3	3	7	13	-6	3
Torquay Utd	**6**	**0**	**2**	**4**	**2**	**8**	**-6**	**2**

August

Down Memory Lane

Don't worry, I'm not going to bore you with page after page of history – you probably get enough of that in school already. These tasty bite-size chunks will relate some of the more interesting and amusing events in the club's history. If you memorise the odd one you'll be able to bore the pants off all your mates next time you're at a loose end!

Did you know .... ?

- Torquay United were formed in 1899, but at first were the poorer neighbours of Ellacombe and Babbacombe, both of whom (posh language, eh?) were more successful. In 1910 Torquay United and Ellacombe joined to form Torquay Town. The club finally morphed into Torquay United in 1921 when Babbacombe agreed to merge with them.

- In those days the kit was a very cunning light blue and dark blue - away teams frequently complained that United's players were virtually invisible against the background of sea and sky. Of course when it got dark they stood out like a sore thumb!

- In 1926 the team changed its kit (Thank goodness! The smell was beginning to affect their play) to black and white stripes, and first got its birdy nickname. No, not the Gulls, or even the Lesser Spotted Blue

Crested Warblers, but ..... the Magpies! (the same as that rather less famous club, Newcastle United).

- The club was finally accepted into the Football League in 1927, their first game in Division 3 South being a 1-1 draw against Exeter City. The lower leagues were organised into North and South to make it easier and cheaper for teams and fans to get to away games – there were no motorways in those days.

- Torquay's greatest FA Cup win came against then mighty Leeds United on a Wednesday afternoon in January 1955! After drawing 2-2 away at Leeds, Torquay won the replay 4-0 in front of a crowd of over 11,000! We can only guess at how many kids mitched off school at lunchtime to go to Plainmoor. Our special researcher I. L. Fynditt has managed to unearth these absence notes from local schools of the day:

Tip-Top United Hit Leeds 4-0

Herald Express headline from the day

Windy Heights
Beans Lane
Torquay

Dear Miss Pomp,

I'm sorry Ronny missed school yesterday afternoon. He tells me he nodded off during History before lunch, then apparently sleep-walked all the way to Plainmoor, where he awoke to find himself standing on the terraces. He tried his best to get out, but the crowd was packed so tight that he had to wait till the end of the match.

Yours respectfully,

Belinda Bobbelem

PS Is there any way you can make History lessons more exciting to try and make sure that this doesn't happen again??

26 Goblin Grove
Torquay

Dear Mrs Sploggitt,

Billy was absent from school yesterday afternoon due to tripping over the cat and bumping his head on the sideboard when he came home for his dinner. He begged to go back to school in the afternoon but I felt it was safer to keep him at home.

In case you're wondering, he didn't go anywhere near Plainmoor.

Yours sincerely,

Tasha Trimp (Billy's mum)

---

367 Blister Street
Torquay

Dear Mr Bashem,

Freddy was off school yesterday afternoon due to a gas leak in our kitchen while I was cooking his fish for dinner. The gas man said we had to get out of the house cos it was about to blow up, so I thought it best to get as far away as possible. Anyway, while we was on the way to my nan's in Barton we bumped into Freddy's Uncle Bert, who said we could stay with him for a few days till it was all sorted out. Bert works as a steward down at Plainmoor, so unfortunately we had to stay there with him all afternoon till he finished his shift. As a result Freddy may have a bit of a sniffle today on account of the cold weather. Please make him use his hanky when he blows his nose, as I'm getting fed up of cleaning it all off his sleeve. Ta.

Yours,

Doris Splinge

If you think that Plainmoor these days can hold 6,400 fans, imagine what it must have been like at the 4th Round match against Huddersfield Town a few weeks later, when 21,908 people managed to squeeze in! Scientists have worked out that if every one of those people took just three mouthfuls of pasty, the added weight would have been enough to cause the stands to collapse and the whole of Torquay to sink below sea level, resulting in catastrophic flooding of the Torbay area and

a great many very damp socks. Legend has it that Mrs Elsie Blott, who lived on Marnham Road, rented her loo out at half-time for 50p a pee, and made enough money to emigrate to Spain and start up her own public toilet outside Barcelona's Nou Camp stadium.

• In United's best ever League season of 1956/57 their average home gate was 8014! They were unbeaten at Plainmoor all season, scoring 7 goals on three occasions, including a 7-2 hammering of Millwall, who then went on to thrash us 7-2 in the return fixture four months later!

• In those days it was traditional to play a team home and away on Christmas Day and Boxing Day! In 1956 Torquay travelled all the way up to London to play Brentford on Christmas Day, then hosted them down here on Boxing Day. How on earth did blokes manage to persuade their wives to let them travel to an away game on Christmas Day!?! They must've spent the first 356 days of the year thinking up a decent excuse!

• You're probably old enough to remember the last-day dramas of recent years (the incredible 3-2 win at Barnet that kept us in the league in 2001, the heart-breaking 1-2 defeat at Colchester that sent us down on goal difference in 2005). In 1957 though, as a taste of things to come, United had to win their last game of that season to gain promotion to the old Division 2 (today's Championship). A draw would be enough if rivals Ipswich didn't win. Ipswich kicked off 15 minutes earlier and won 2-0 against a weakened Southampton team. Torquay, trailing 1-2 at Crystal Palace, stormed forward in search of the two goals they needed, but all to no avail. No play-offs then either, so that was that for another year.

United finished level on points with Ipswich, but in those days these issues were decided not by goal difference, but by goal average (it didn't change till 1976). Basically, the number of goals you scored was divided by the number you conceded, so it finished:

    Ipswich   101 divided by 54 = 1.870370

    Torquay   89 divided by 64 = 1.390625

We missed out on promotion by 0.4797454!

- 1962 saw the Gulls battling relegation from Division 3 (the present Division 1) on the final day of the season (sound familiar?). Just like last season they only needed a point to be safe, whereas their opponents Barnsley needed to win to avoid the drop. At 2-1 up things looked to be going our way, but three unanswered goals saw United go down 2-4 and suffer the heartache of relegation back down to Division 4.

Barnsley finished the season with 38 points compared to Torquay's 36, but that was in the days when a win was only worth 2 points. Under today's system of 3 points for a win, United (W15, D6, L25), would have ended with a total of 51 points, the same as Barnsley (W13, D12, L21). They both had goal differences of -24, but United would have survived, having scored 76 goals to Barnsley's 71. Cruel, eh?

- Maybe the club's greatest FA Cup adventure took place in January 1965, when United were pulled out of the hat to play Spurs. Another crowd over 20,000 at Plainmoor saw the Gulls come back from 1-3 down to score twice in the last few minutes through Robin Stubbs, and almost snatch a win when they hit the bar with a header in the final minute.

> *Wacker Remembers .... the Spurs replay*
>
> Alan 'Wacker' Smith played for the Gulls as a wing-half, centre-half and full-back between 1958 and 1967, before a knee injury sadly ended his playing career.
>
> *"We went up to London on the train - a bit of a treat as we normally travelled to away matches by coach. The weather that day was terrible, absolutely chucking it down, but when we got to White Hart Lane we learned that the groundsmen had taken the covers off the pitch at lunchtime. Of course the pitch became waterlogged during the afternoon and the game had to be called off. We all had to get back on the train and go home again! Spurs had a few injuries to key players that day, and there were mutterings that they'd wanted to have the game postponed so they could get those players fit before they played us again. Some fans reckoned they were scared of us!*
>
> *We went back the following week and booked into the Kensington Palace Hotel - the absolute height of luxury for us small-town players! On the night we eventually went down 1-5. I remember I had the job of marking their tricky, speedy right-winger, Terry Dyson. He didn't figure in any of their goals, so I suppose I must have done a fair job on him. It was just great to play against huge stars such as Jimmy Greaves, Dave Mackay and Alan Gilzean in such a fantastic stadium in front of 50,000 fans. It was probably the highlight of all our careers."*

- United made their first appearance on Match Of The Day in 1968, when the cameras were at Plainmoor to witness a 3-0 victory over local rivals Exeter City.

- The club record for consecutive wins was set in 1998, with eight on the trot against Shrewsbury, Hartlepool, Brighton, Hull, Doncaster, Chester, Lincoln and Chelsea (only joking, it was Cardiff really).

- 1985. Torquay finished bottom of Football League. Oops. Fortunately no automatic relegation at that time. Survived. Least said the better. Let's move on shall we .....

- 1986. Finished bottom of Football League. Oops. Fortunately no automatic relegation yet. Survived. Least said the better. Let's move on shall we .....

- Saturday 5th May 1987 could certainly claim to be the most dramatic afternoon ever at Plainmoor. That year the FA had introduced automatic relegation for the club finishing bottom of Division 4. Torquay went into the match 23rd, a point above Burnley but a point behind Lincoln (at that time only one club went down). With United 0-2 down to Crewe at half-time, Burnley winning but Lincoln losing, the situation was desperate: we needed to score at least twice to get the point that would save us and send Lincoln out of the Football League on goal difference.

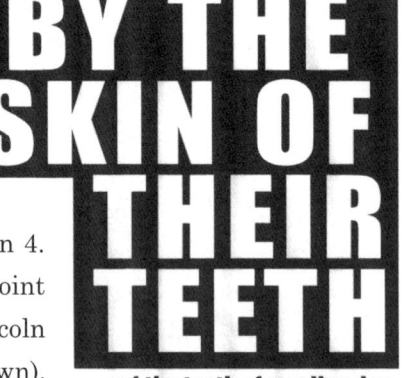

– and the teeth of a police dog
Herald Express headline

A Jim McNichol goal just after the restart gave the crowd hope, but the real drama was reserved for the last few minutes. In an atmosphere that can only be described as frenzied, United, spurred on by a wildly screaming crowd, piled forward as if their very lives depended on it.

Feeling left out of the action, Bryn the police dog clearly decided his time had come for instant fame. Perhaps he'd missed his lunch, but he certainly didn't miss United skipper McNichol. As Jim went to take a throw-in, Bryn took a firm bite on what we might politely call his upper thigh (well it is a kids' book after all!). On came the medics to see to an understandably tearful Jim, resulting in four minutes of injury time. And would you believe it, in the fourth minute of injury time Paul Dobson seized on a loose ball, knocked it into the back of the net and hauled United back from the brink of disaster.

In the resulting pandemonium Bryn was led away, but when tracked down later he barked: *"I feel I must apologise for my actions. I don't know what came over me. Being colour blind I clearly mistook Jim for one of the Crewe players. However, I'm glad that it all turned out well in the end. By the way, I must say I found Jim rather tasty, though a pinch of salt wouldn't have gone amiss."* *

Can You Believe That??? (1)

On the last day of the 1961/62 season, Northampton Town needed a win away at Halifax to stay in the Football League ..... and send Halifax down into non-league football. Going into injury time the score was 0-0 and the Halifax fans were just beginning to heave a sigh of relief and start to think about where they were going to celebrate after the match. But Northampton staged one last-gasp attack, winger Terry Bull getting to the bye-line and swinging in a cross which seemed to be sailing harmlessly over the bar and away for a goal kick.

Enter stage left Pecker, manager Eddie Ball's pet budgie, who had escaped through the open front room window and followed the team coach all the way to Halifax. Swooping down from the roof of the away stand, he threw himself heroically into the path of the ball and deflected it with his beak into the top left-hand corner, out of the despairing reach of the Halifax keeper......... P.T.O

* *Translation by Mr Al Satian.*

> The crowd went wild, Northampton stayed up, Halifax were relegated, and Pecker picked up the Creature of the Match award (it was a silver watch, which wasn't a great deal of use to him, though he did like to sit on his perch and admire his reflection in its face). When interviewed in his cage the next day he chirped: "*When the chips are down it's up to every member of the club, mammal, fish or bird, to do their bit. I would've been sick as a parrot if we'd gone down, but instead I'm as perky as a Pecker can be.*"
>
> **Strange but true!!! Or is it???** *(find out on page 155)*

A fitting way to end our stroll down Memory Lane. Who knows what dramas lie ahead for the faithful fans. At least you can pretty much guarantee one thing: life for a Gulls fan is never going to be boring!

My prediction is that the year 2112 is going to be a dream year for United. The previous 4 seasons will have seen promotion up through the divisions until they arrive at the Premiership in 2115.

Gazing into my crystal ball I clearly see the following results in the first 3 months of the season ('the Gulls score is always first, so 2-0 is a win but 0-1 is a loss):

CHELSEA	(h)	3-1
ASTON VILLA	(a)	2-2
CARLISLE	(h)	4-0
MAN Utd	(a)	1-2
LIVERPOOL	(a)	1-2
SPURS	(h)	3-2
READING	(a)	0-0
ARSENAL	(a)	1-3
LEEDS Utd	(h)	2-0
WEST HAM Utd	(h)	3-3
EVERTON	(a)	1-0
WIGAN ATHLETIC	(h)	3-0
NEWCASTLE Utd	(a)	2-3
MAN CITY	(a)	2-0
MACCLESFIELD	(h)	5-1

I know there are some unexpected names in that lot (Chelsea still up there??), but 2115 is a long way off and football's a funny old game!

Now complete this table for United following those results:
(Remember it's 3 pts for a win, 1 for a draw!)

	P	W	D	L	F	A	GD	Pts
T.U.F.C.								

Football in The Community Leader Frank Prince ran a penalty shoot-out at St. Marychurch last week in which 34 children took part.

They each took five penalties. At the end two children, Billy and Betty, had scored all five penalties, so they went into a sudden-death shoot-out. They each scored with their first three efforts, but Billy's fourth penalty hit the bar and bounced out, whereas Betty's found the bottom corner of the net.

How many penalties were taken altogether?

If two goalies shared the work equally, how many penalties did they face each?

All football matches are obviously 45 minutes each way, with a quarter of an hour for half time. Torquay's evening game against Rochdale was due to kick off at 7.45, but was actually three minutes late starting. At the end of the first half there was 2 minutes of added time, and at the end of the match 4 minutes.

What time did the final whistle blow?

..... and what would that be on a 24-hour clock??

R	T	O	D	I	S	P	R	E	N	T	A	L	E	N
I	P	R	O	F	J	E	V	U	R	K	G	A	B	S
C	U	R	E	N	R	A	G	S	B	W	E	S	P	I
V	Q	T	S	P	N	L	R	I	L	M	O	D	U	D
I	N	I	O	S	R	E	I	T	A	Y	L	O	R	L
G	E	D	W	B	S	O	M	A	P	U	D	O	G	E
H	Y	E	L	K	C	O	H	D	N	R	O	W	H	O
O	M	A	S	A	K	E	L	T	E	C	A	U	Y	E
U	E	T	R	O	W	O	I	D	S	E	M	R	U	A
F	M	G	F	L	G	O	Y	O	S	Y	R	O	G	S
O	Y	O	E	B	T	R	U	I	A	M	T	C	H	S
U	E	T	J	M	H	T	L	L	R	N	I	T	I	J
N	T	B	B	A	R	L	E	D	W	U	F	A	L	W
D	?	G	S	L	I	F	R	O	S	Q	F	L	L	R
Z	K	A	E	V	T	E	P	R	O	H	T	E	B	S

There's one! only joking!

In the grid you'll find these United players

GARNER   TAYLOR   HILL
VILLIS   HEWLETT   WOODS
HOCKLEY   EVANS   THORPE

Names can go in any direction, including diagonally! Beware! Some letters may be used in more than one name!

Can you spot the question? If so, what's your answer? And don't tell me any fibs, cos I'll find out!!

29

Look at this diagram of a football pitch....
then test your multiplication skills with the
questions on the page opposite.
I've rounded up some of the measurements to make it a
bit easier for you. (Yes, you're right, I'm too kind!)

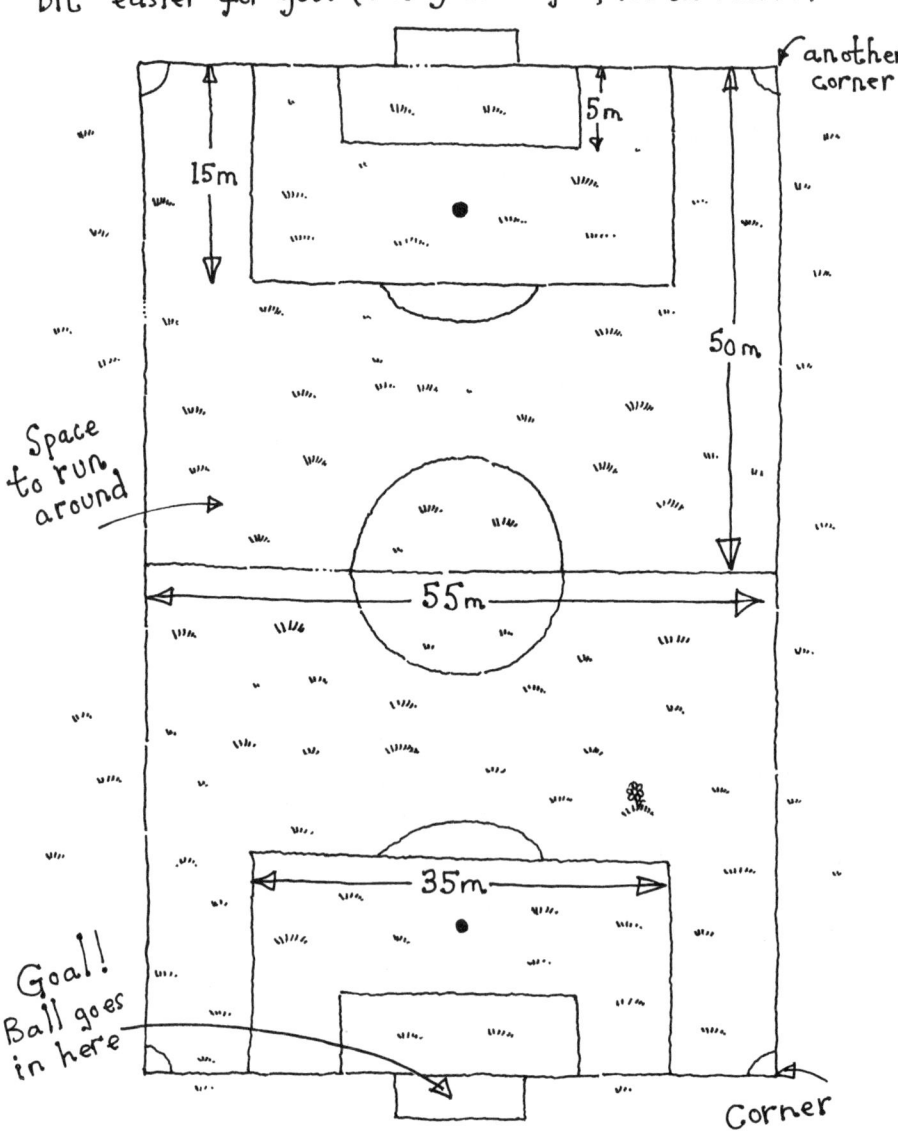

AB'S TIP!

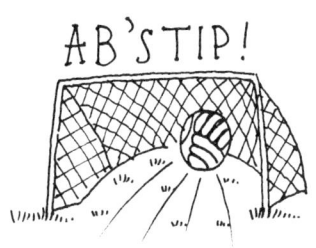

To calculate the area of a rectangle you multiply the length by the height. So to find the area of this shape you would do

$6 \times 3 = 18$

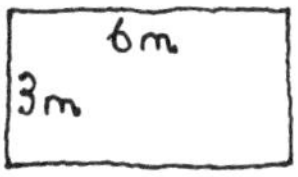

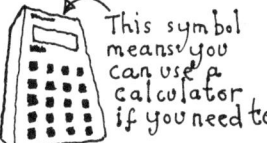

Write the answer in square metres (m^2)

This symbol means you can use a calculator if you need to!

WHAT'S THE AREA OF THE PENALTY BOX?

WHAT'S THE AREA OF THE WHOLE PITCH?

During a training session the players do shuttle runs. Starting from the goal line they go:

- To the 5m line and back 10 times.
- To the edge of the penalty box and back 5 times.
- To the halfway line and back 3 times.
- To the other end of the pitch and back twice.

HOW MANY METRES DO THEY RUN ALTOGETHER?

Due to a typesetter with an evil sense of humour (me!) 10 words have been left out of this match report from 2013. I managed to track them down and have written them underneath.

CAN YOU WORK OUT WHERE THEY GO AND PUT THEM BACK IN THEIR PLACES, PLEASE??

Twenty coachloads of Gulls fans made the long trip down to Barcelona for the club's first ever European match last night. The home team were so .... that they decided to leave superstar Ronaldinho on the bench, whilst Torquay put out a strong defensive team, playing a 4-5-1 .... with Thorpe on his own up front.

United were put under .... from the off, and went a goal behind when Eto'o got the better of Woods in the air to send a header .... over everyone and in off the far post. Things went from bad to worse when Garner had to leave the field with a calf injury just before half-time.

The second half followed a .... pattern to the first, with United on the back foot for long spells. Needing a second goal Barcelona sent on Ronaldinho after an hour, and .... heroic defence United went two down ten minutes from time. A mazy dribble by that man Ronaldinho ended when he was brought down by a .... Hockley tackle. The Brazilian took the spot kick himself and coolly slotted the ball into the bottom corner, sending the keeper the .... way.

With the game nearing the end Torquay needed a miracle, and it arrived when a defensive mix-up let in Thorpe. He used his strength to break free and then .... the ball over the stranded keeper to give United a vital away goal.

The return leg at Plainmoor is already sold out, though the whole match will be shown live on a .... screen in Castle Circus. Get there early!

YOUR MISSING WORDS ARE:
lobbed similar pressure giant desperate formation
despite confident   wrong looping

32

LAST WEEK THE PLAYERS DID A WEIGHTS SESSION IN THE GYM TO HELP INCREASE UPPER BODY STRENGTH.......

Steve Woods was doing bicep curls, working with a 25kg weight. He did 10 curls then had a short rest before doing the same thing 3 more times.
HOW MUCH DID HE LIFT ALTOGETHER?

TOTAL Kg

Kevin Hill used a lighter weight but did more repetitions. He did 15 curls each time with a 20kg weight.
HOW MUCH WEIGHT DID HE LIFT IF HE DID FIVE SETS OF CURLS?

TOTAL Kg

Matt Hockley did 6 different weights exercises, and after each exercise he did some sit-ups. He did 100 sit-ups the first time, then 90, then 10 fewer each time after that!
WHAT WAS HIS TOTAL NUMBER OF SIT-UPS?

TOTAL

smarty pants

really heavy, lifty thing!

September

There's one main reason why most kids hate September. Back to school! Is there a more depressing thought than that?

Who invented school anyway? Probably some sadistic teacher. They're all the same - torturers in drab, creased clothes, who take great delight in making your lives a misery for nine whole horror-filled months of the year. Every morning you get dragged out of bed at some ungodly hour, despite your claims to have:

- a raging fever

- a violent allergy to wool which will make you come out in a terrifying, livid rash if you're made to wear your school uniform

- a belly-ache so fierce that just the mention of a school dinner will cause you to challenge the world distance record for a projectile vomit

- plague (Black Death is the favourite cos everyone's heard of it and its name has maximum scare impact)

- all of the above (only try this one if all else fails, or if your parents are totally pathetic!)

Evenings that had recently been spent dozing in front of the tele or playing football in the street, are now filled with pointless boring homework tasks that you know your teacher will never mark (they only give them out because their single aim in life is to bring heartache and despair to everyone under the age of eighteen).

Anyway, where were we? Ah yes, September. We all hoped and prayed that after such a depressing August at the club, the only way was up. In fact, to go downwards from bottom of the Football League would be a major challenge to any club. Well, the way the month started, it looked as if United were going to manage to achieve that most difficult of tasks. Things actually DID get worse!

First blow: Leroy had been hoping to fix a loan deal for the young Southampton striker David McGoldrick, but as time ran out before the transfer window closed the Saints decided at the last minute to keep him.

Second blow: Defender Brian McGlinchey finally gave up on his fight against his niggling back injury. It was decided that the only long-term answer was an operation, which would rule him out for the rest of the season.

Third blow: The injury to Buster Phillips meant that he wouldn't be back in action for another seven weeks!

Fourth blow: Alex Lawless played against Shrewsbury, but was then sidelined until the middle of October. A real injury crisis was developing.

Fifth, sixth and seventh blows: In the middle of all this, United made the long trip up to Rochdale and got hammered 4-1. Craig Taylor got sent off for what was judged to be a deliberate handball. Richard Hancox, coming on as sub in his first league game for nine years, suffered abuse from a section of United's travelling fans. Understandably upset, he responded with a less than polite gesture and was afterwards fined under the club's disciplinary code.

Meanwhile, the club's three French players were coming under pressure from fans (someone always ends up taking the stick, usually unfairly, when a team is on a bad run). There was talk of a ban on French being spoken during training sessions - there's always a danger that any foreigners will get isolated from the locals, so communication between the two camps is vital. Making all the English players speak French could have been another way around the problem, and might well have been more amusing, but this option was unfortunately never tried. Mind you, as most Brits find a French accent almost impossible, that's probably just as well ......

And then it happened (cue drum roll).... wait for it! ..... could it be?? .....
YESSS! GET IN THERE! WE WON!!!

September 10th was that great day, with Shrewsbury Town the visitors to Plainmoor. Despite changes due to their injury crisis (Kevin Hill at left-back!) United took the lead after barely a minute when Alan Connell thumped an unstoppable drive in off the bar. After a Shrews equaliser, Darren Garner got on the end of an inviting Mamadou Sow cross in first half stoppage time to send the Gulls in one up, and that's how it stayed. United's first victory of the season at their ninth attempt. Alleluya! It didn't take us off the bottom, but surely it was the kick-start to the season we'd all been waiting for.........

And carried on waiting for, as it turned out, because a week later we went up to Grimsby and were thumped 3-0. Ouch!

In an effort to get everyone behind the team, a 'Yellow Day' was planned for the home match against Lincoln. If it was yellow for Torquay, it was a red and blue day for the visitors. Blue because they lost after being 1-0 up at half time (United's goals again coming from Connell and Garner), and red because in one of the most bizarre finishes in recent years, Lincoln had three players sent off in the last twelve minutes. The most comical was the dismissal of the goalie, Alan Marriott (no relation to Andy), who was clearly just a tad miffed about the ref's decision to send off full back Morgan, who'd just done his best to kick Alan Connell over the stands into Warbro Road. You could tell Mr Marriott was upset, because he sprinted from his goal, out towards the corner flag, and tried to take off poor Alan's head by blasting the ball at him from three yards away - while he was still hauling himself back up off the ground! Truly a mad moment, and a memorable end to a remarkable match, which saw United shoot up to the dizzy heights of 22nd, at long last out of the relegation places.

It would be nice to say that the recovery continued with another positive result at Leyton Orient in the last game of the month, but unfortunately the ending was a sad one. The Gulls put up a good fight but Jo Kuffour's goal wasn't enough to stop them going down 1-2, Leroy's post-match comments suggesting that the ref might have done a little better (see below). We were back on the bottom.

With Sako by now also struggling with an injury, Leroy brought in the first of a group of loan signings. Alan McAliskey joined on a month-long deal from Huddersfield Town to ease the striking problem. Would he provide the missing link? Would United's fortunes take a turn for the better?? Would we finish October off the bottom??? Would there be fewer questions at the end of the next chapter????

Only time would tell.

> **September Quotes:**
>
> *"When you're successful it's down to hard work, and it's the same when you're not. There's absolutely no chance of me throwing the towel in."*
> **Only a month into the new season, and Leroy is already under pressure to resign from some fans after the defeat at Rochdale.**
>
> *"You come all this way, and at least you want a referee who is fair. He shouldn't be allowed to do the game. He should be doing park football.*
> **Leroy shows his annoyance following the loss at Orient.**

September Stats

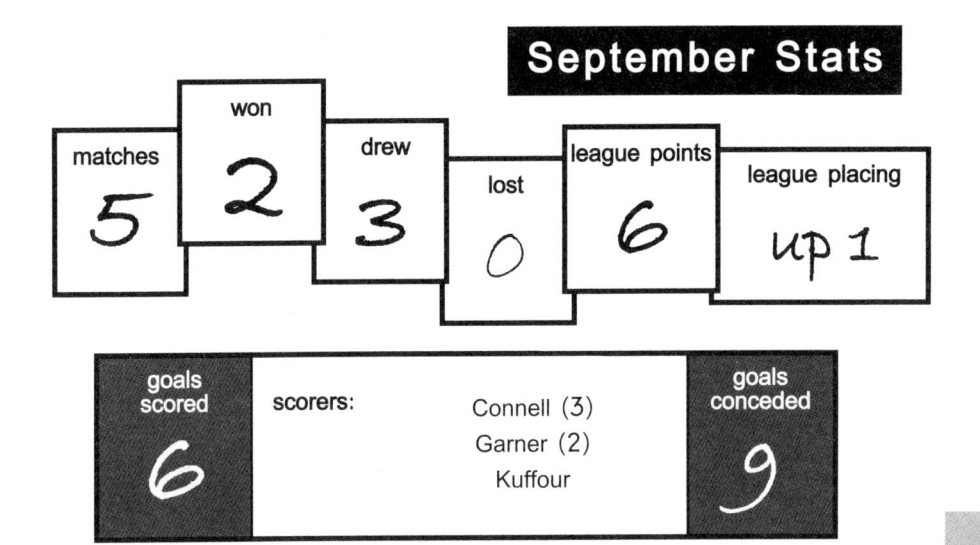

- matches: **5**
- won: **2**
- drew: **3**
- lost: **0**
- league points: **6**
- league placing: **up 1**

- goals scored: **6**
- scorers: Connell (3), Garner (2), Kuffour
- goals conceded: **9**

- players used: **20**
- average match time in possession of ball: **43%**
- yellow cards: **11**
- red cards: **1**

fouls — by United: **52**, by opponents: **64**
goal attempts — by United: **56**, by opponents: **69**

total attendance: **15,073** (Ave: **3,015**)
total miles travelled: **1,676**

Table at end of September

	P	W	D	L	F	A	GD	Pts
Grimsby Town	11	7	2	2	18	8	10	23
Wycombe W.	11	7	2	2	22	12	10	21
Chester City	11	5	5	1	20	11	9	20
Leyton Orient	11	6	2	3	18	17	1	20
Rochdale	11	5	2	4	20	13	7	17
Northampton	11	4	5	2	17	12	5	17
Cheltenham	11	4	5	2	16	13	3	17
Oxford United	11	4	5	2	14	13	1	17
Notts County	11	4	5	2	11	12	-1	17
Shrewsbury	11	4	4	3	13	10	3	16
Lincoln City	11	3	5	3	13	11	2	14
Darlington	11	3	5	3	14	13	1	14
Peterborough	11	4	2	5	11	11	0	14
Carlisle United	11	3	4	4	14	15	-1	13
Wrexham	11	3	4	4	12	13	-1	13
Bristol Rovers	11	3	3	5	12	18	-6	12
Rushden / D.	11	2	5	4	11	17	-6	11
Barnet	11	3	1	2	8	7	1	10
Stockport C.	11	1	7	3	15	18	-3	10
Boston United	11	1	7	3	14	19	-5	10
Macclesfield	11	2	4	5	13	19	-6	10
Bury	11	2	3	6	10	16	-6	9
Torquay Utd	**11**	**2**	**2**	**7**	**8**	**19**	**-11**	**8**
Mansfield T.	11	1	4	6	15	21	-6	7

WHO AM I??? (1)

In each of the boxes you'll find four facts about a player, plus one clue (I really am too good to you!) All you have to do is identify the player!

I was born in Torquay in 1982.

One of my nicknames is Tyrone.

My favourite TV programme is Only Fools And Horses.

I'm keen on fishing in my spare time.

Clue: Has played his whole career at Torquay

My name is ....

I'm a Devonian, born 1974   I like to listen to Cold Play

My all-time favourite footballer is Roy Keane

Before a game I always put my left boot on first!

Clue: Only ever scored 4 goals for the Gulls

My name is ....

As a child I supported Liverpool (favourite player Steven Gerrard)

I'm 22 years old.   I'm a useful cricketer.

My favourite band is 50 Cent.

Clue: 191cm (6 feet 3 inches) tall

My name is ....

October

Lots of people have told me they like October, but for the life of me I've never really understood why. Maybe it's the start of those crisp dark nights when you can see your breath dancing in the air as it's freed from your mouth, and the stars twinkling like tiny diamonds in the necklace of the jet black sky. Maybe it's ……….. sorry! Please forgive me, I've just had an attack of poetry. It's a disease left over from my long-ago schoolteacher days, which occasionally strikes without warning. I'll be all right after a glass of water and a lie down. If it happens again, give me a good slap and tell me to get a grip.

So, October. By now you've settled into the dismal prison camp routine that is daily school life. You've probably had your first detention / warning letter / savage beating. Your stomach has come to terms with the diet of slop and cardboard (hopefully it's getting used to school dinners as well). You've realised that your early dreams of escape are just that - dreams. You get put off the idea when you gaze out of the window during yet another stunningly boring Science lesson, only to catch sight of the grinning heads of the last attempted escapers impaled on the railings as a grim warning to others. Hmm, now there's an idea ……

"Don't worry lads... that only happens to the teams that beat us!"

No, the only bright spots as far as I can see are the half-term holiday and the chance to egg your teachers' windows and front door at Halloween, and you've got to wait thirty whole days for that treat.

....

Everything seemed to be going so well for United when Alan Connell's second-half strike, his fourth goal in six games, gave them victory at Cheltenham in their first game of the month. United's 20 goal attempts to Cheltenham's 7 shows how well the team went forward and took the game to their opponents. On top of that a clean sheet is always welcome (have you checked yours recently??). The win moved us up to 21st in the league, and most fans and reporters were saying that the bad days were now behind us and we were going to shoot up the table like a rat up a drainpipe. Hopefully a win at home to Barnet on the Friday night would confirm that.

Unfortunately, that was as good as it got in October. If you don't like horror stories you'd best skip the rest of this chapter - you won't be able to sleep tonight. The Barnet game was about as boring as life gets on the football pitch. I'm told that doctors had to treat 14 head injuries as fans fell asleep on the spot and keeled over in the stands. The club was contacted by the National Insomniacs Society asking to supply them with a video of the match, and the game went straight in at number 2 in the 50 Most Boring Activities chart (just above 'Watching your dad paint the back garden fence', and only pipped for the top spot by 'Being dragged round the shops with your mum looking for new shoes on a Saturday afternoon').

The only positive that came out of the game was the point that took us a place higher in the league, but don't get excited cos the slide back down again was soon about to start.

Everyone's patience, already wearing thin, was stretched even more by the farcical episode of 'The Mystery of the Disappearing Russians.' Actually they were Belarussians, FC Smena Minsk, over in UK to support their national team who were playing Scotland. They'd thought it would be a jolly idea to play a match while they were here (speaking little English, they were probably fed up trying to make any sense of Eastenders and Big Brother with the sound off). Naturally they chose to come to the sunny English Riviera and give us a game. Except that they didn't. Apparently some of their players got 'involved' with some Scottish fans (or police, depending on which version you listened to) so they decided to go straight home instead. Thanks for letting us know, comrades! Another friendly was hastily arranged instead, but with all due respect, Newton Abbott doesn't quite have the same exotic ring to it as FC Smena Minsk.

A 2-4 away defeat at Wrexham meant that the next home game against fellow strugglers Macclesfield was a bit of a must win game if we were to start to climb out of trouble. In the end it was only Connell's cracking volley that allowed us to escape with a point from a 1-1 draw. Still, that was the first sign that United had the fighting spirit to be able to come from behind and get something out of a game. It would stand them in good stead in the following months.

Sandwiched between those two matches, the LDV Vans Trophy had driven in, parked briefly, then driven off again after a 1-3 defeat to Swansea in front of only 1,025 fans.

As if things weren't bad enough, rumours started to go around that Bristol Rovers were lining Leroy up to take over as their new manager. When the Chairman gave him a few days off to "recharge his batteries," many of us wondered if he was on his way out of Plainmoor. Assistant Coach Richard Hancox took over training, but couldn't prevent a strong United line-up crashing out of the Devon Cup with a 0-1 home defeat to Dawlish Town. On the night Dawlish were fantastic, proving once again that the gap between Division 2 and the non-league game is nowhere near as great as some people might think.

The final nail was hammered into the October coffin by Boston United, whose 2-0 win nudged Torquay back down into the same place they'd started the month. Rock bottom. Not to worry, things were bound to pick up. Weren't they?

> **October Quotes:**
>
> *"Our supporters were absolutely immense. They helped us a lot, from before the first whistle to after the last, and I can't give them enough credit."*
> **Leroy is full of praise for the travelling fans who cheered the team to their 1-0 victory at Cheltenham.**
>
> *"In terms of entertainment it was very poor. The referee was very poor too, and all in all it made for a terrible spectacle."*
> **Leroy accurately sums up the Barnet bore draw.**
>
> *"We're not enough of a threat up front. In the last third we're hoping things happen rather than making them happen."*
> **Leroy's verdict after the Boston defeat was to prove true for much of the season.**

October Stats

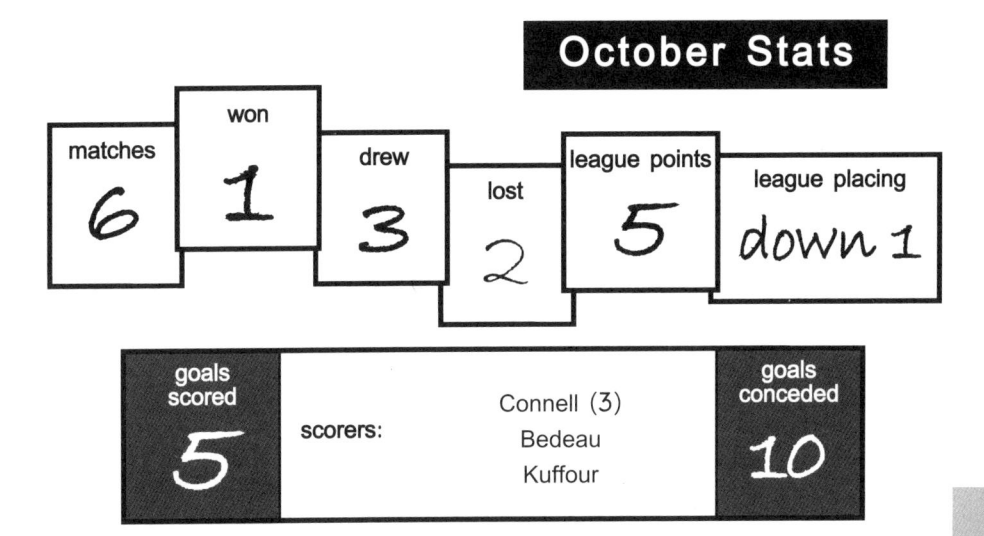

matches	6
won	1
drew	3
lost	2
league points	5
league placing	down 1

goals scored: 5
scorers: Connell (3), Bedeau, Kuffour
goals conceded: 10

players used	17
average match time in possession of ball	50%

yellow cards	red cards
10	0

fouls	by United	by opponents
	60	78

goal attempts	by United	by opponents
	61	56

total attendance	total miles travelled
16,444	1,338
Ave: 2,741	

Table at end of October

	P	W	D	L	F	A	GD	Pts
Leyton Orient	16	9	4	3	25	20	5	31
Wycombe W.	16	7	9	0	30	18	12	30
Grimsby Town	16	8	4	4	21	10	11	28
Rochdale	16	8	2	6	30	21	9	26
Chester City	16	6	7	3	30	22	8	25
Carlisle Utd	16	7	3	6	20	16	4	24
Wrexham	16	6	5	5	22	18	4	23
Northampton	16	5	8	3	20	16	4	23
Boston United	16	5	8	3	22	21	1	23
Peterborough	16	6	4	6	21	16	5	22
Oxford United	16	5	7	4	15	15	0	22
Notts County	16	5	7	4	15	19	-4	22
Darlington	16	5	6	5	18	16	2	21
Shrewsbury	16	5	6	5	18	20	-2	21
Cheltenham	16	5	5	6	18	22	-4	20
Lincoln City	16	4	7	5	18	17	1	19
Bristol Rovers	16	5	4	7	19	25	-6	19
Bury	16	4	5	7	17	21	-4	18
Barnet	16	4	6	6	17	23	-6	18
Mansfield T.	16	4	4	8	26	25	1	16
Rushden/D.	16	3	6	7	16	23	-7	15
Stockport C.	16	2	9	5	22	32	-10	15
Macclesfield	16	3	6	7	16	26	-10	15
Torquay Utd	**16**	**3**	**4**	**9**	**12**	**26**	**-14**	**13**

October

Training

Are you one of those kids that needs to be dragged kicking and screaming out if his warm, cosy bed in time for lunch during the summer hols, by a mum who claims that she's already:

1. hoovered the whole house

2. scrubbed the bathroom

3. done three loads of washing (and ironed the lot)

4. cleaned out the pets

5. fed the pets

6. taken the hamster to the vet after it sicked up all its nuts

7. done the shopping

8. made breakfast for all your goody-goody sisters

9. washed up and dried all the dishes and ......

10 still found time to SAVE THE PLANET FROM A DEVASTATING METEOR STRIKE!!!

If so, you might want to skip this chapter.

Or .... are you one of those intensely annoying kids who leaps out of bed as soon as his Donald Duck alarm clock quacks him awake at the ungodly hour of 6:30, does 50 press-ups, has a bracing cold shower, bounds downstairs to make his own breakfast of muesli and low-fat yoghurt, then drags his clearly reluctant dog on a 5-mile jog, beaming at everyone he meets and calling out to anyone who'll listen: "Smashing day, isn't it!" while cheerfully whistling the tune to 'Oh What a Beautiful Moooorning!' at maximum volume? If so, this chapter's for you! (even if you *are* mad as a hatter)

It's possible that one of those morning dog-walks might've taken you to Oddicombe Beach, by the cliff railway. If it did, you may have been puzzled by the sight of grown men in blue track suits sprinting energetically up and down that steep hill beneath the trees, while normal humans trudge along, dragging a dog that appears to have lost the will to live. Thoughts probably flashed through your mind as you edged away from them: lunatics on the run from a local asylum? Auditions for a new TV series of Boot Camp? Slightly odd characters fleeing from an improbable invasion by giant squids? The truth is much more simple. TUFC's pre-season training has begun.

Assistant Coach **Richard Hancox** *(right)* gave us this insight into last season's training programme at the club.

Players normally report for training mid-July (it was two weeks earlier in 2005 due to the 2006 World Cup, which meant an earlier start to the season). They've had a break for the best part of two months, but most will have kept themselves in good shape - they're professionals who know that if they let their standards slip they may soon be looking for another job.

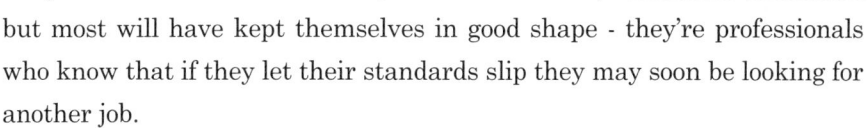

Training correctly is a difficult balancing act. Players need to be match fit by the opening day of the league season in August, then stay match fit until May. It's easy to get the impression that players slog their guts out on the training ground every day of the week to make sure they're fit enough to last the pace on a Saturday. But that amount of hard training could well lead to a player being too tired to perform at the weekend, or put so much strain on muscles and joints that they pick up injuries much more often.

"Isn't it great to be paid to do a job you love!"

Most of the really hard work is put in during those first few weeks leading up to the opening league game. The first two days will consist of a run. That's it. Phew! .... For an hour! Doh! After that training will be geared more towards other aspects of fitness and performance:-

- shuttle runs and other agility activities will improve speed off the mark and speed on the turn, which are both vital in a match no matter what position you play.

- rugby-style ball-handling games are introduced which help with teamwork, support play and movement off the ball. Only being allowed to score with your head makes it more challenging, as well as developing heading skills.

- small-sided games will usually start in the second week back. A typical game would be 8-a-side on a 60 x 40m pitch (like playing across one half of a pitch), using full-sized goals, for 45 minutes. This is gradually building up to a realistic match situation, improving stamina, helping new players get to know team mates and helping the coaches to suss out levels of fitness and performance.

- around this time the coach will want to start sorting out his best playing combinations. What's his best back four? Which midfield players combine best with each other and have the right blend of skills (it's no use playing four bruisers who can't pass, or four playmakers who can't tackle!) Which attacking players have the best understanding? How can we get a mix of left and right sided players?

Once he's got what he thinks are answers to these questions, those players will be given more chance to work together. For example, it's vital that a defensive unit is comfortable together. The two centre-backs need to have an almost telepathic understanding - they have to be able to read each other's movements as well as their opponents'. This only comes from long hours of playing alongside each other, both in training and matches. At the same time it's no good if the whole defensive formation falls apart when one player is injured. Other players need to be slotted into the system during training, so that they are ready if called on to step in.

- set-piece plays at free-kicks and corners will be rehearsed. Who's going to take the corners? From both sides? In-swingers or out-swingers? What signals will we use? One hand raised might mean a near post ball, two hands a far post ball, a handclap might be an in-swinger right under the crossbar, or maybe an out-swinger towards the penalty spot. A finger up the nose may either mean a low driven ball to the edge of the six-yard box, or a really stubborn bogey that's been lodged up your hooter since before the game and urgently needs shifting.

Of course other teams aren't daft - they all have their own set plays. So the defence has to practise together to be prepared for opposition corners. Do we have a player on each post? What if the centre forward tries to block the goaly by standing on his toes? Who goes to the near post to defend against flick-ons? If they take a short corner, who goes out and who stays in? Who picks up the players making runs from outside the box? Everybody has to know his job like the back of his hand, and fringe players need to know all the jobs in case they have to come on as left-back, right-back or centre-back. How often do you see a goal conceded from a corner and a goaly going absolutely berserk with a player because he didn't do his job properly? (It's nearly always the goaly who does his nut - they're never to blame for anything!)

Pre-season friendlies are necessary, but mean a difficult balancing act for coaches. Players can be 'training fit' after two or three weeks, but need four or five games to be fully 'match fit.' It doesn't matter how much training you do, the demands of a match are different. The opposition are giving 100% to beat you, tackles are flying in, you're going for a full 90 minutes and you may be battered and sore for part of that time. The non-stop concentration, the tension and the adrenalin flow all tend to affect energy levels.

The pre-season matches provide the players with an important stepping stone to the first game of the season. The coach will be making last-minute adjustments to tactics and formations, as well as trying out different players in a variety of positions. 'Tinkering,' you might call it.

Although obviously useful, pre-season adds four or five more games to an already busy schedule. In the lower divisions where squads tend to be smaller and so player rotation rarer, the coach has to guard against player burn-out. He doesn't want half his squad jaded or out injured by Christmas.

Once the real season starts, and players get into the swing of matches every Saturday and regularly on Tuesday evenings, the fitness aspect of the training sessions is scaled down. Players need time to recover from the knocks and fatigue from the last Saturday, and need to be full of energy and raring to go for next Saturday. A typical morning session will start at 10:00 and finish at 11:30. After a warm-up jog players will go into a series of fitness/agility drills before moving onto possession and skills activities. The goalies will have taken themselves off for a while to practise on their own. The session will usually finish with set-piece moves from corners and free-kicks, or maybe some shooting practice.

When John Cornforth took over from Leroy he immediately increased the amount and the nature of the training. As he said at the time: *"They're professional athletes as well as footballers, so there's no way they can train for just an hour and a half; they've got to work hard for longer than that."*

The squad had a more varied programme during the week, with more work in the afternoons. Partly this was to improve fitness levels, which he felt was one of the reasons for the previously disappointing results, and partly it was to keep the players on their toes, preventing them from getting into a training rut. One of the most noticeable changes in those first weeks of Corny's management was the increased work-rate of the players in matches, giving the opposition much less time on the ball, causing them to rush their passes and leading to mistakes.

Some managers will announce their team at the end of training on the Friday. Players will probably already have a pretty good idea of who's in and who's not, due to the practice matches and drills they've just been doing. The idea behind this method is that they are then able to relax a little and concentrate on the job they know they're going to have to do the next day. Leroy generally worked this way.

Some managers prefer to keep players guessing, and don't announce their team until shortly before the match on the Saturday afternoon. This was Corny's method, the thinking being that the whole squad would make sure they were 100% ready physically and mentally on the Saturday afternoon, just in case they were in the team.

If you visited all 92 league clubs, you'd probably find 92 different ways of training and match preparation. Different hours, different drills, different intensity, different atmosphere, different diets, etc etc. There's no right way or wrong way - it depends on the personality and style of the coaches as well as the changing needs of a changing group of players throughout the season. And in ten years time these routines may have changed completely. As Alan Smith's recollections show, football is an ever-changing game:

Wacker Remembers........ training and match preparation.

Alan 'Wacker' Smith played for the Gulls as a wing-half, centre-half and full-back between 1958 and 1967.

"In the 60s we used to do our training at Plainmoor. We'd do laps of the pitch for warm-ups, and sprint up and down the terraces time after time for speed and stamina.

Once a week we'd run to Maidencombe and back along the coast path - a distance of about 6 miles. It was always very competitive - no-one wanted to be the last man back!

We used to meet before every home game at the Trecarne Hotel in Babbacombe at 12 o'clock. We'd have lunch together there - lots of the lads would have steaks, but I remember my favourite used to be poached eggs on toast followed by rice pud!

The boss would hold the team talk at the hotel, then we'd all drive or walk to the ground in time to get changed, rub some liniment into our legs then get out on to the pitch at five to three, just in time for a quick warm-up before kick-off."

ANY GOOD AT CROSSWORDS?
Prove it!!
(All the answers are connected with football)

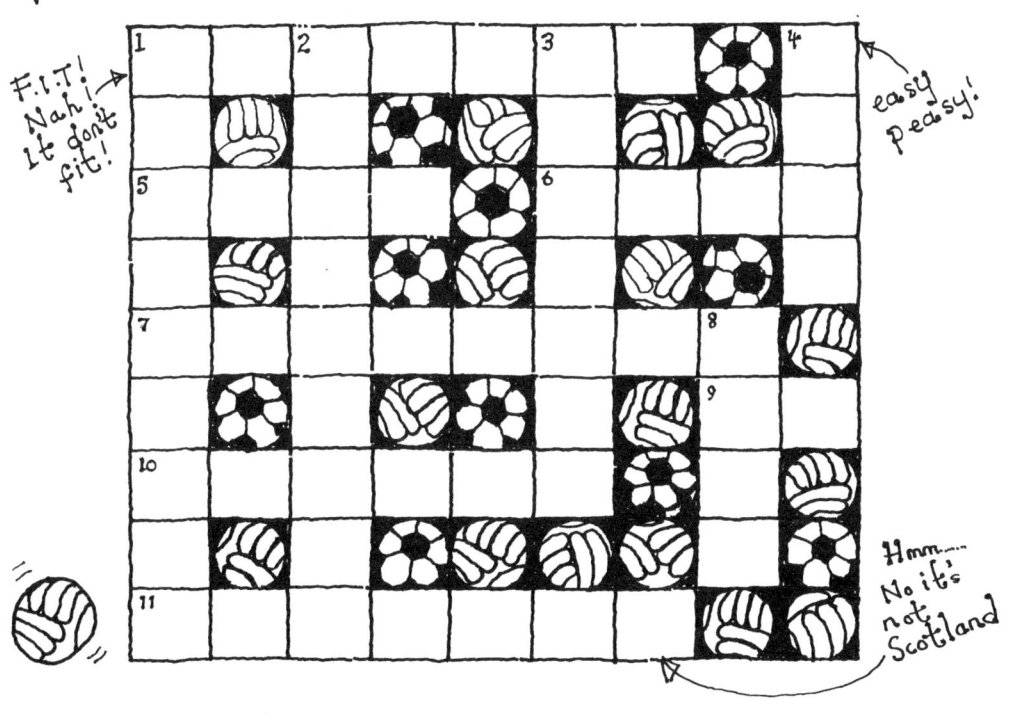

F.I.T.! Nah! It don't fit!

easy peasy!

Hmm... No it's not Scotland

ACROSS
1. Players might get this from eating meat or eggs. (7)
5. This links Lawless, Ferguson and Russell. (4)
6. A striker may get a yellow or red card for this. (4)
7. A defender may stand here for a corner. (two words, 4 4)
9. You really don't want to score one of these! (2)
10. You might have these on your hot dog at half time. (6)
11. Glasgow and Queens Park are. (7)

DOWN
1. Our ground. (9)
2. A serious injury might need one. (9)
3. A 5-a-side tournament might be played here. (7)
4. This kick could be indirect. (4)
8. Huddersfield or Grimsby? (4)

Gulls manager Ian Atkins needed to pick two strikers out of Thorpe, Ward, Phillips and Hill for the game against Barnet.

HOW MANY DIFFERENT PAIRS COULD HE CHOOSE FROM THESE FOUR?

← Players' pegs Arrgh!

| THORPE | WARD | PHILLIPS | HILL |

TOTAL

LATEST NEWS: Mickey Evans passed a fitness test and is now available for selection too.

EVANS

HOW MANY DIFFERENT PAIRS COULD HE CHOOSE NOW??

TOTAL

The typesetter (me!) is such a dunce that 11 spelling mistakes have crept into this match report.

Can you help me by finding them and writing the correct spellings underneath, pleeeease?...

> A huge crowd filled Plainmoor to the brim for Torquay's FA Cup 6th round clash with Premiership table-toppers Arsenal. United were forced to make three changes to their starting line-up after injuries to Thorpe, Phillips and Hewlett. They had obviously desided that attack was their best chance of getting a result because they pressed forward right from the first whistle. Evans forced a corner in the forth minute and Woods thundered a header just over. When Garner ratteled the Arsenal bar with a 20-yard piledriver United looked to be getting well on top. As the half war on the visiters came more into the game and Taylor had to make exellent last-ditch tackles to deny Henry and Van Persie.
>
> In the second half Arsenal began to gain the upper hand, and it was no great suprise when they went ahead. Villis blocked a Campbell header on the line but was helpless to prevent Cole smashing in the rebound. As the final whistle neared United started to poor forward in search of an equaliser. Hockley bought a fine save from Lehmann. Thorpe fired a shot just wide and Garner had a goal ruled out for offside. When all seemed lost, deep into added time Hill rose above the defence to power an unstopable header into the roof of the net. Arsenal won't forget their visit to Plainmoor in a hurry, and will need to improve in the replay if they are to privent Torquay reaching their first ever FA Cup semi-final.

....

....

....

....

ANAGRAMS

An anagram is a word in which all the letters have been muddled up. Can you un-muddle these to get the right words??

YOU MIGHT BUY THESE AT THE GROUND:

fasrc _____ ubgrre _____

siphc _____ rmroepgma _____

YOU CAN SEE THESE ON THE PITCH:

erreefe _____ asrbrsco _____

lerfgconar (2 words) _____ _____

THESE TOWNS OR CITIES ALL HAVE CLUBS IN DIVISION 2.
Can you identify them?....
Unfortunately some of the letters have been missed out! (aah! shame!)

__tt_____am   __rl_n__on

_oc_d__e   _a_s_i_l_

_et___or___h   __r___

naughty naughty!

Ian Atkins decides to have some training grids marked out in one half of the pitch at the Racecourse, so it looks like this:

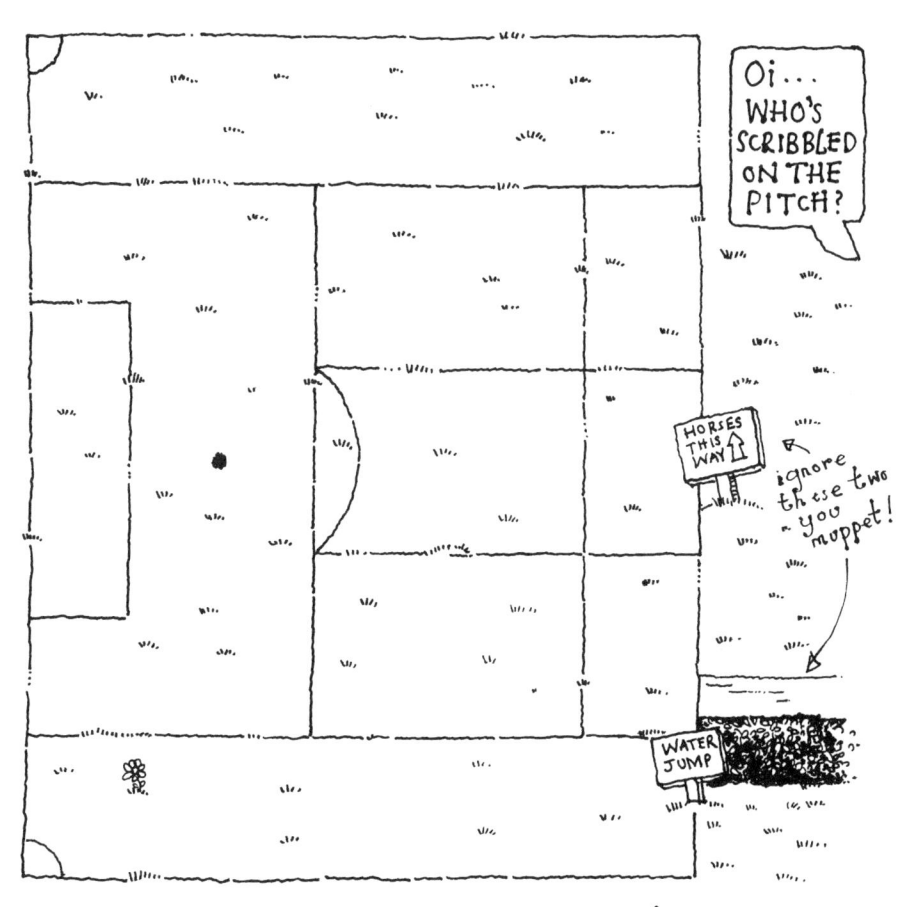

Oi... WHO'S SCRIBBLED ON THE PITCH?

HORSES THIS WAY

ignore these two ~ you muppet!

WATER JUMP

How many rectangles can you find altogether in the diagram??

TOTAL

USING MY CRYSTAL BALL TO GAZE INTO THE FUTURE, I SEE GREAT CHANGE IN FORTUNES FOR THE GULLS.....

Following their takeover by Russian billionaire Nikolai Avgotanich, United have made steady progress up the leagues, and arrive in the Premiership in 2012.

Look at this section of a league table from the 2013 season. With 8 games to go we're right up there challenging for a Champions League spot.

	P	W	D	L	F	A	GD	Pts
Aston Villa	30	14		2	57	34	23	56
Reading		15	7	8	49	32	17	
Torquay Utd	30	15	6	9	51	29		51
Man Utd	30		14	4	55	27	28	50
Everton	28	12	11	6	48	36	12	
Arsenal	29	11	10	8	42		14	43
Newcastle Utd	29	11	9	9		29	12	42
West Ham Utd	30	10		10	42	33		40

As you can see, 10 numbers have gone missing. (Have you checked under the cushions on the settee? That's where most things end up!) Can you use your mathematical brain to put them in?

November

So, half-term's been and gone and you're now back on the treadmill. You've got Bonfire Night to look forward to - treacle toffee, baked spuds, bangers, pretending the guy blazing away on the top of the fire is really your PE teacher, etc etc. But once that's over there's only the distant view of Christmas on the horizon to keep you going. If you're lucky you might be doing football in Games this half-term. If you're unlucky it'll be either hockey (getting whacked on the hand by a hard wooden stick in sub-zero temperatures) or rugby (getting trampled into the mud by some gorilla with an attitude problem and a grudge).

My advice is: just hang in there. Once you get into December it's all downhill - carols, fun Christmassy activities, parties and presents. So don't lose the will to live. Grit your teeth and force a smile when your teacher decides no-one can go out to play football at break because she thought she felt a raindrop an hour and a half ago and she doesn't want to risk anyone catching a chill (by now the sun's beating down out of a cloudless blue sky).

November was another difficult period for the Gulls - played 5, won 0. Starting the month at the foot of the table, many thought that the football we were playing deserved better, that our luck would surely turn, and that a dramatic rise up the table was just about to happen. Alas, it was not to be.

Speculation about Leroy's possible move to Bristol Rovers ended abruptly when they appointed Lenny Lawrence and Paul Trollope as their management team. The waters of Leroy's future remained muddy, however, when it emerged that the Costa Rican national team had their eyes on him as the coach to lead them towards the next world cup. Leroy had played one game for them back in his youth, and admitted that he felt strong ties with the country. These ties must have felt even stronger when a number of Torquay 'fans' seemed to be leading a campaign to have him sacked, and Chairman Mike Bateson had to close the message board on the website following a series of abusive messages.

On the pitch it was a case of hellos and goodbyes. French import Mamadou Sow was soon packing his bags, exported back to France. Nicky Skinner also left the club, and four others were put on the transfer list - Leon Constantine, Darren Garner, Morike Sako and Carl Priso. Constantine was soon snapped up, moving to Port Vale on loan. In return, in came a batch of loan signings to add fresh blood and energy to the season. Ian Stonebridge (Wycombe Wanderers), Anthony Lloyd (Huddersfield), Adam Lockwood (Yeovil Town), Paul Robinson (York City) and Craig Woodman (Bristol City) all arrived. Training sessions must have been a little confused at first: "Watch yer back, er .... tallish bloke with the short fair hair!" or "Great ball, little fella with the funny northern accent!"

Mind you, things could have been worse ... but not much. The tone for the month was set right from the very first match, an FA Cup tie at home to Harrogate Town of the Nationwide Conference North. Not a very romantic or money-spinning draw, but at least one that suggested we should cruise through to the second round without too much difficulty. However, confidence had been dented by recent results, and when the visitors went ahead after 20 minutes it seemed that a shock might be on the cards. The team again showed that they don't give in easily though, and threw everything at Harrogate in the second half. Goalie Price kept them in front with a string of fine saves, but something had to give, and it was Ian Stonebridge, on his debut, who finally grabbed the equaliser ten minutes from time with one of United's best goals of the season. A replay all the way up in Yorkshire was not a prospect Leroy would have looked forward to, given the injury problems still affecting the first team.

The frustration continued the following weekend when a remarkable game saw the Gulls go down 3-4 at home to Carlisle. The afternoon had begun badly when the ref called the two captains together for the toss-up, only to find that he'd forgotten to bring a coin out with him! Picking up a blade of grass he hid it in one fist, asking the visiting captain which hand it was in! Whatever next!? Maybe he could get them to play stone-scissor-paper, or do eeny-meeny-miny-mo??? Once the game got underway United managed to come from behind three times, including two goals from debut striker Paul Robinson and Kevin Hill's first of the season. But all the hard work proved worthless when Carlisle scored a late winner following a controversial free kick. Leroy was so incensed by the decision

"Sorry lads... I spent all my dosh on my pre-match pasty!"

that he strayed outside his technical area to complain - a sending off offence. He was sent off. (To hear his plain, honest opinion of the ref's performance, take a look at 'November Quotes' below)

A further defeat at Barnet meant the only league point came from the 2-2 draw at Notts County - and that the result of an injury time equaliser from Jo Kuffour. Thankfully the other clubs down among the relegation swamp didn't manage to swim to safety, and so we kept in touch with Macclesfield, Mansfield, Rushden and Diamonds and Stockport.

The only real ray of sunshine was the eventual progress through to the 2nd Round of the FA Cup, when the Gulls finally saw off Harrogate 6-5 on penalties in the replay after the game finished 0-0. Not for the first time Andy Marriott was the hero, saving two penalties and then slotting home the sudden-death decider from the spot. Once again the veteran goalie was proving his priceless value to the club.

All in all then, a disappointing November. Started bottom, finished bottom. But not tailed off yet, and most observers reckoned we were playing football far too good to go down. Leroy was putting the right messages across and the team was getting the ball down and playing a clever passing game, rather than hoofing the ball upfield and hoping a big striker could get on the end of it. A few more goals and more solid defensive displays, and maybe we could look forward to a Happy Christmas after all.

> **November Quote:**
>
> *"He's going to get nought in my report. You could've got someone off the street to do it a hundred times better!"*
> **Leroy clearly wasn't impressed by Gary Lewis's refereeing skills after the Carlisle game.**

November Stats

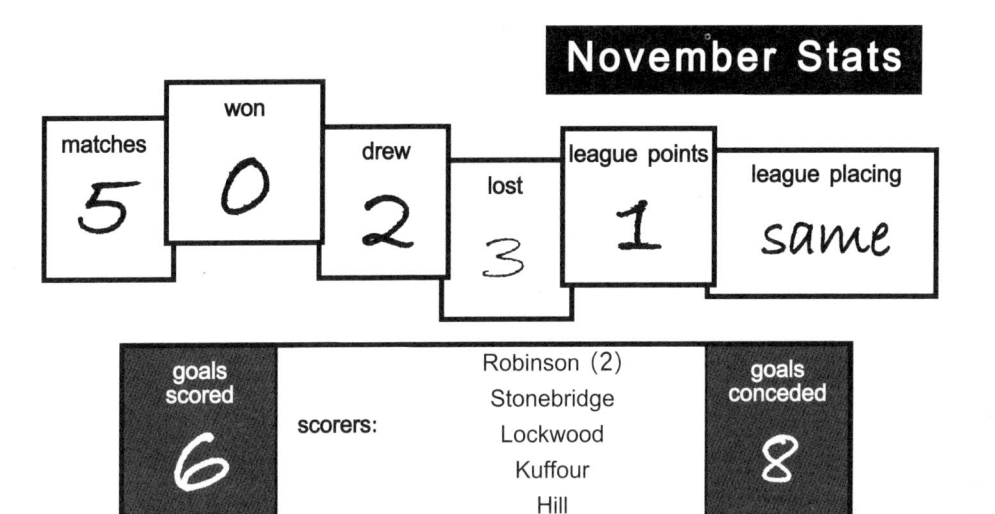

- **matches**: 5
- **won**: 0
- **drew**: 2
- **lost**: 3
- **league points**: 1
- **league placing**: same

- **goals scored**: 6
- **scorers**: Robinson (2), Stonebridge, Lockwood, Kuffour, Hill
- **goals conceded**: 8

- **players used**: 18
- **average match time in possession of ball**: 48%

- **yellow cards**: 7
- **red cards**: 1

- **fouls**: by United 55 | by opponents 84
- **goal attempts**: by United 67 | by opponents 49

- **total attendance**: 14,558 (Ave: 2,912)
- **total miles travelled**: 1,576

Table at end of November

	P	W	D	L	F	A	GD	Pts
Wycombe W.	19	9	10	0	35	20	15	37
Leyton Orient	19	9	7	3	28	23	5	34
Grimsby Town	19	10	4	5	28	16	12	34
Rochdale	19	10	3	6	38	27	11	33
Chester City	19	7	9	3	35	25	10	30
Carlisle Utd	19	9	3	7	26	21	5	30
Cheltenham	19	8	5	6	26	25	1	29
Northampton	19	6	10	3	25	17	8	28
Wrexham	19	7	6	6	27	21	6	27
Boston United	19	6	8	5	25	25	0	26
Notts County	19	6	8	5	21	25	-4	26
Peterborough	19	6	6	7	24	21	3	24
Darlington	19	5	8	6	20	19	1	23
Oxford United	19	5	7	7	18	23	-5	22
Shrewsbury	18	5	7	6	22	25	-3	22
Bristol Rovers	19	6	4	9	22	32	-10	22
Barnet	19	5	7	7	20	26	-6	22
Lincoln City	19	4	9	6	21	23	-2	21
Bury	18	5	5	8	20	22	-2	20
Mansfield T.	18	5	4	9	28	29	-1	19
Rushden/D.	18	4	7	7	18	24	-6	19
Macclesfield	19	4	7	8	18	29	-11	19
Stockport C.	19	2	11	6	26	37	-11	17
Torquay Utd.	**19**	**3**	**5**	**11**	**17**	**33**	**-16**	**14**

WHO AM I??? (2)

As long as you haven't skipped Part 1 you'll already know what to do, so I won't waste my time telling you again. If you did skip Part 1 then go back and do it, you slacker. You should be ashamed of yourself!

My interests include golf and cricket.

As a kid I was a Man United fan.

I was born in Exeter 30 years ago.

My favourite programme is Dream Team

Clue: Brilliant header of a football.

My name is ....

My nicknames include Baldy and Fatty!

I love bangers and mash.

My favourite band is Faithless.

I'm from Plymouth and I'm pretty old!

Clue: Midfielder, signed from Rotherham.

My name is ....

A 30-year-old Bristolian, I used to play for Bristol City

I'm a bit of a DIY man about the house.

My favourite meal is Spag Bol.

I like to spend free time playing with my son.

Clue: Scored one goal last season.

My name is ....

Will it, won't it? Matt Hewlett looks on anxiously to see if his goal-bound effort will make it over the line .... the picture below shows he had nothing to worry about!

This was United's second goal against Bristol Rovers (their only two goals in six games in August!), and put them into a 2-0 lead. Unfortunately, late lapses saw their dreams shattered as they crashed to a 2-3 defeat.

A masterclass in shooting technique.

Note the body control, not trying to hit the ball too hard. The eyes are focused on the ball and the arms are used to help balance.

Notice also how the body leans back more when hitting a sidefoot shot, to try and place the ball more accurately, as shown by Darren Garner (left) and Liam Coleman (right) ......

......but needs to be more upright with the weight forward when hitting a driven shot, to make sure the ball doesn't sail over the bar and into someone's garden in Warbro Road! Demonstrations of this by Tony Bedeau (above), Matt Hockley (above right) and Kevin Hill (far right).

CB

CB CB

How to be a Headbanger: get up high - good knee bend provides maximum spring. Again, arms are used for balance (defenders sometimes push down on the shoulders of attackers - this is naughty). Eyes stay glued on the ball, though often close at the last moment, as Woodsy demonstrates below.

CELEBRATION TIME!

Clockwise, from bottom left:

Tony Bedeau demonstrates the **High Punch** *and the more restrained* **Cool Fist**.

Alan Connell's repertoire includes the **Single Arm Raise**, *the* **Two-Finger Salute** *and the dramatic* **Roar**.

Quiet man Paul Robinson prefers the **Shhhhh**.

Photos: Colin Bratcher

(above) Torquay's most familiar legs??? Frankie Prince with Matt and Justin, United's Football In The Community team. Helping to train the young stars ot the future, Frankie runs courses for 5-12 year olds in the evenings and during school holidays. Any boys or girls out there who want to start out learning the game, improve your skills and fitness or simply enjoy playing football? Give the team a ring on **01803 322551**.

(left) Just who **is** Gilbert the Gull???

a) On-the-run bank robber Charlie 'Chainsaw' Bobbins, hiding from police after his daring 2004 raid on NatWest in Barton?

b) Once promising starlet Gilbert Geoffrey Gulliver, now living in shame and unable to face the public following his last-minute open goal miss against Exeter in 1998?

c) Bert Noggis, 43, of Hartop Rd, St Marychurch,who left home (without telling his wife Doris) to travel to Carlisle for the away match in 2001. Despite returning to Torquay three weeks later he has yet to pluck up the courage to go home and face her.

d) None of the above, they're all a load of tosh.

Who **is** this United player behaving in such a disrespectful manner towards the cameraman???

(Below) Richard Hancox is helpless to prevent Dezzy Duck's right wing shot putting Ark Athletic one up on Lake Plainmoor. Coach Noah fielded a 2-2-2-2-2 formation which clearly baffled their human opponents.

(Right) Ref Iain Williamson's shout of "Boo!" is perfectly timed to put Jo Kuffour off his shot.

Sack the photographer!

Being a clumsy halfwit, I dropped my camera down the toilet at half-time. Now I can't work out who I've taken photos of!

Can you help???

(answers p159)

December

As soon as December arrives most of you can start to relax. It's all downhill from here. Tests are usually over, and teachers have their eyes on the staff party and a nice long holiday, blissfully undisturbed by irritations and annoyances (ie children). For your part you can look forward to such stimulating educational tasks as:

1. making and writing Christmas cards

2. writing letters to Santa (PS: Please can you find time to make my teacher disappear/explode/come out in a plague of boils. Come on Santa, you can do it!)

3. making a sparkly mobile to hang in your bedroom (yeh right! Like frogspawn, only a tiny percentage survive - odds on it'll end up in the classroom bin)

4. colouring in any number of pictures of the nativity/robins/snowmen/reindeer, etc. You won't go far wrong if you follow this simple December tactic: if it moves, colour it in. If it isn't moving, kick it till it moves, *then* colour it in! Just another little tip here: try to use as many different coloured thick felt tips as you can lay your hands on - firstly it

guarantees maximum messiness on the paper, secondly it bugs the hell out of the teacher (this is *always* a bonus).

The only possible clouds on the horizon are the Carol Service and Nativity Play. The first can generally be avoided by deliberately singing way off key in any rehearsals (not too difficult for most of you, probably). If you're also brave enough to stand in the front row and give it full, eyes-bulging top volume, then believe me, instead of your teacher's desperate plea of: "We really want all of you to do everything you can to be in church for the service tonight," you're more likely to hear: "You don't want to risk catching a chill coming out on a cold December night, Billy. Isn't there something you'd rather stay in and watch on tele instead?"

For you younger readers, a Nativity production isn't quite as simple to get out of. By the age of eleven your nativity acting career probably already consists of: shepherd, back end of donkey, sheep (twice), at least one King/Wise Man, and if you're a real teacher's favourite Joseph or Mary. These two special parts are reserved for kids who will not

a) pick their nose and wipe the bogey on their robe, or ....

b) pee themselves uncontrollably after ten minutes on stage.

You might try constantly forgetting your lines, but beware, this isn't an easy trick to pull off if you're an innkeeper whose total script reads:

> Joseph: Have you any room for a weary traveller and his heavily pregnant wife, after such a long and tiring journey?
>
> Innkeeper: No. *(closes door)*

Even teachers aren't that stupid ..... are they??

As Christmas approached, Leroy's letter to Santa may have included the following wish list:

1. a win
2. another win
3. i-pod
4. yet another win. Like socks, you just can't have enough wins!
5. Roy Keane. He'd left Man Utd - maybe he had a long-lost granny in St Marychurch that he wanted to spend more quality time with?? Then again maybe not, cos he joined Celtic instead.
6. FA Cup draw away to Man Utd / Chelsea / Arsenal / Liverpool. Think of what we could do with all that lovely cash!
7. Jumbo-sized bottle of headache pills
8. Train set. (sorry, I was getting it mixed up with *my* list!)

If you'd looked into a crystal ball on the first of December and told Leroy we'd go through the whole month without being beaten, he'd probably have jumped for joy, then suggested you go and get your head examined. But that's exactly what happened - 3 wins and 3 draws in all competitions, 13 goals scored and off the bottom of the table at last.

The month got off to a great start when two goals from in-form striker Tony Bedeau powered United to a fantastic 2-1 victory over Notts County in the FA Cup. This was followed on the Sunday afternoon with the news that the club had been drawn at home against Premiership club Birmingham City in the fourth round. Ok, it wasn't quite the money-spinner that Man United or Chelsea would have been, but nevertheless a guaranteed full house at Plainmoor and some dosh to spend on new players. When the BBC announced that they'd be paying the club £15000 to show highlights on Match of the Day, it must have stretched the grin on Chairman Mike Bateson's face even wider.

Back on the pitch, Bedeau was again on target against Northampton in

December

the first of two thrilling 3-3 draws. It was Kevin Hill who was the hero though, popping up in the last minute to earn the Gulls a vital point. The game will be remembered most however for a refereeing howler that cost us dearly. Ref Lee Probert had already blown for a foul outside the box when Scott McGleish went through to put the ball in the net. The game automatically stops when the ref blows his whistle, but instead of bringing play back for a free kick, he allowed the goal to stand, much to the amazement and anger of the fans (and Leroy, whose blood pressure must have been off the scale by then!). An official apology afterwards was very nice, but two points would have been much better received. Yet again we were left with the sour taste of frustration in the mouth at the final whistle.

By now the pattern of United's matches was becoming predictable: the opposition would always score (usually more than one), we would move heaven and earth to score more than they did, and one of the teams would come up with an equaliser or winner in the last few minutes. When Oxford came down to play, both teams obviously read the script and rehearsed it all week, because the Plainmoor crowd were again treated to a see-saw 6-goal epic. Kevin Hill netted twice as the Gulls fought back to claim a draw, and the 3-3 result meant that the lucky faithful had witnessed 22 goals in the last four home games!

Exciting though it was for the fans, these draws were doing nothing to pull United clear of the relegation dogfight. They needed wins. Their first of the month, (and their first win at Bristol Rovers since 1947!) came thanks to a last-gasp clincher from Monsieur Sako. Things were definitely looking up, especially as the three points lifted us off the bottom for

> A Liverpool fan and an Everton fan are in front of the firing squad. The officer asks if they have any last requests.
> **Liverpool fan**: Before I die, I'd really like to watch a video of our Champions League Cup Final win against Milan in 2005.
> **Officer**: Ok, I think I can arrange that. (turning to Everton fan) What about you? Do you have any last requests?
> **Everton fan**: Yeh. Shoot me first!

Joke!

the first time since October. At long last we could look down on somebody worse off than us!

And so we came to Christmas Day. Lie-in, open presents, plateful of turkey with all the trimmings (does anybody truly like sprouts, and if not why do they return to plague us every year?), Christmas pud, Harry Potter film, few drinks, fall asleep in front of the TV ...... Actually no. With a game against top of the league Wycombe Wanderers on Boxing Day, the players were out training as usual on Christmas morning - one of the drawbacks of being a pro footballer.

For the first half against Wycombe it looked as if the tide had well and truly turned. Our boys clearly hadn't had too much turkey or whisky because they came out of the tunnel like a yellow tornado. Goals from Sako and Bedeau saw them 2-0 up at half time and playing like kings. Unfortunately Wycombe had other ideas, and two second half goals meant that the draw felt like two precious points dropped rather than one point gained.

Still, recent results had left the team unbeaten in six and full of confidence, and they would have relished the chance to do battle with fellow strugglers Stockport County. County had not only lost 6-0 against Macclesfield on Boxing Day, but they'd sacked their manager the next day too. They looked ripe for the picking! Despite the hassle of such a long journey during the Christmas period, players and fans travelled north in eager anticipation. The almost five-hour trip flew past as everyone chatted about how many we'd score, and how rosy the future was starting to look. Meanwhile, outside the warmth of the coaches and cars, the temperature plummeted to sub-zero. The pitch froze, the referee decided it was unplayable, and everyone had to turn round and drive all the way home again. What a pain! In case you were wondering, the only compensation Torquay got for the wasted journey was that Stockport had to pay for our team hotel when we went back up there for the rearranged match. Doesn't seem fair, does it?

That left only one game left in 2005. On New Year's Eve United took on Rushden and Diamonds in a real bottom-of-the-table clash. A win was crucial, so the joy and relief were obvious when Jo Kuffour swivelled and smashed a right-foot thunderbolt into the top corner in only the second minute. When Kevin Hill dived to head a second just before the interval it all looked done and dusted. Game over. The nerves began to set in after the break, however, and in the end we had to hold on desperately in a nail-biting last ten minutes for a 2-1 win. The victory leap-frogged us above Rushden into 22nd place, and meant that fans and players alike could go out and celebrate the New Year with a bit more hope in their hearts. We were sure that 2006 was going to be our year. It certainly couldn't be as bad as 2005, could it! Or was I opening my big mouth too soon?!? (what do you mean, "Not for the first time"???

> **December Quotes:**
>
> *"Is that all you got me?? One pathetic jumper you know I'll never wear cos I'll look a complete pratt, a box of Maltesers past its sell-by date and a Spice Girls CD?!?"*
> **Me**
>
> *"In view of their struggles in the league, I've today offered to loan Wayne Rooney to Torquay United for the rest of the season. Well, it is Christmas after all!"*
> **Sir Alex Ferguson enters into the Christmas spirit.**
>
> *(sorry, I made that one up!)*

December Stats

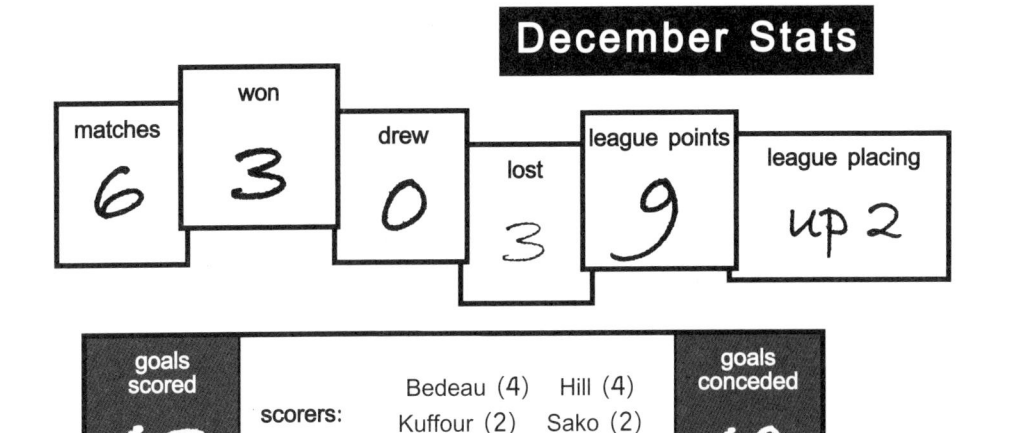

- matches: **6**
- won: **3**
- drew: **0**
- lost: **3**
- league points: **9**
- league placing: **up 2**

- goals scored: **13**
- scorers: Bedeau (4), Hill (4), Kuffour (2), Sako (2), Lockwood
- goals conceded: **10**

- players used: **19**
- average match time in possession of ball: **48%**

- yellow cards: **4**
- red cards: **0**

- fouls by United: **67**
- fouls by opponents: **115**

- goal attempts by United: **79**
- goal attempts by opponents: **79**

- total attendance: **19,557** (Ave: 3,260)
- total miles travelled: **730**

Table at end of December

	P	W	D	L	F	A	GD	Pts
Wycombe W.	25	12	12	1	48	28	20	48
Grimsby Town	24	14	4	6	39	20	19	46
Leyton Orient	25	12	7	6	40	32	8	43
Carlisle Utd	24	12	5	7	36	25	11	41
Cheltenham	25	11	7	7	32	29	3	40
Northampton	24	9	11	4	31	21	10	38
Wrexham	24	9	7	8	36	28	8	34
Chester City	24	8	9	7	38	32	6	33
Rochdale	24	10	3	11	43	42	1	33
Peterborough	24	8	8	8	29	24	5	32
Bristol Rovers	25	9	5	11	30	39	-9	32
Darlington	24	7	10	7	29	26	3	31
Boston United	24	6	12	6	27	28	-1	30
Lincoln City	25	6	12	7	29	31	-2	30
Barnet	25	7	9	9	26	32	-6	30
Notts County	24	7	9	8	24	32	-8	30
Oxford United	24	7	8	9	27	30	-3	29
Macclesfield	24	6	10	8	30	34	-4	28
Bury	22	7	6	9	25	26	-1	27
Mansfield T.	24	7	6	11	36	39	-3	27
Shrewsbury	23	6	8	9	27	31	-4	26
Torquay Utd.	**24**	**5**	**8**	**11**	**28**	**42**	**-14**	**23**
Rushden/D.	24	5	7	12	23	39	-16	22
Stockport C.	23	2	11	10	26	49	-23	17

The Fizzy O!

Sorry, I just ran that through Spellcheck and it's come up with a correction:

The Physio!

Q. *What does your dad do if your car makes an odd, ugly burping noise every time he changes gear?*

A. Well, if he fancies himself as a bit of a self-taught mechanic, he might have a good look at the engine, maybe play around with a spanner or two and get it back on the road with a smug smile on his face ...... then spend two hours in Sainsbury's car park waiting for the AA man, watching black smoke pour out from under the bonnet and trying to convince his very cross wife and kids that this latest problem had nothing at all to do with his botched repair job.

Or .... he can phone up the garage and get the experts (you hope!) to fix it properly.

Q. *What does your mum do if you wake up in the morning with the feeling that someone slipped a handful of sharpened gravel into your bedtime cocoa, and the tooth fairy has spent a happy night scrubbing the inside of your throat with sandpaper?*

A. Well, if she reckons she knows a thing or two about natural cures, she might shovel vitamins down your neck like there's no tomorrow, or concoct evil-smelling herbal brews that stink the whole house out, totally freak out the dog and make cat wee taste like banana milk-shake.

Or .... she can take you to the doctor and get the trained experts to put you right.

Q. *What do you do if your calf muscle starts to tighten up as you push off to chase upfield to support your winger at Friday morning's training session?*

A. Well, let's start with what you don't do.....

You don't pretend you're fine, carry on playing to the end of the session, tell the boss you're really up for tomorrow's important league game then go home and rub some Deep Heat on it, hoping it'll go away.

Why not? You've been in great form recently, you desperately want to play, you fancy your chances of bagging a goal, and you need that win bonus to buy that gorgeous new dress (for the wife, of course).

1. Playing with an injury is putting your season at risk - there's a real chance you'll make it worse and spend weeks, not days, watching from the stands instead of being out there on the pitch.

2. If you have to come off after 10 minutes your boss has to use one of his precious subs and probably change his game plan. If your team loses as a result, all your team mates will miss out on their win bonuses too - they won't thank you for that. You've let them down.

3. When you later let on to the manager that you'd been carrying an injury from training, he's not going to laugh it off with a "Never mind, boys will be boys!" He's going to be waiting for you in his office with a king-sized rollicking.

"*So what's the answer then, clever clogs?*" I hear you ask.

Well, just like in the other two examples, you go and see the expert - in this case the Club Physiotherapist (Fizzy O).

At the start of the 2005-2006 season that job belonged to Kevin Matthews. Only three games in, however, Kevin and the club agreed to 'a mutual parting of the ways.' The new kid on the block, stepping into the vacant post, was **Darren James** *(right)*. We caught up with him after a busy training session at the club's Newton Abbott Racecourse base.

Q. Hi Darren! How did you come to be physio at United?

Well, before you can apply for a job with a football club you need the right academic qualifications. To get on a university physio course you normally require an 'A' Level in Biology at Grade B or above. I went to Bath University, gaining a BSc (Bachelor of Science) Honours degree in Physiotherapy. After that I did a spell of on-the-job training (basically work experience) supervised by an experienced physio. As soon as the vacancy came up at United I jumped at the chance and now here I am!

Q. What does your normal working day consist of?

I arrive at the training ground at 8:45 to unlock and prepare my room. From 9:00 to 1:00 I treat any players who have minor niggles or more serious longer-term injuries. After I've cleared up my own room I clear up in the changing rooms too, then head back to Plainmoor. I write up my notes on the players' injuries and carry out any necessary extra treatment, assessing the players' fitness. If there's an evening game I'll be at the ground at 6:00 to give massage and any last-minute treatment needed before the match.

Q. Some footballers seem to be almost constantly injured. What's the most common injury that you have to treat?

Definitely muscle tears. You may think that a top Olympic athlete puts his leg muscles under enormous strain, but once they're underway athletes move at a fairly constant speed with a regular stride length, whether it's a sprint, middle or long distance. Footballers, on the other hand, spend 90 minutes jogging, walking, sprinting and standing still. They're regularly pushing off from a standing start to sprint 10 metres, turn sharply, then do the same thing again.

[Try doing a 5 or 10 metre shuttle run in your back garden for 2 minutes and feel the pressure it puts on your calves, hamstrings, ankles and knees. Then imagine doing it on and off for 90 minutes, with jumping, tackling, getting knocked over and getting back up again mixed in. That's what a footballer goes through once or twice a week, as well as the training sessions. AB]

Q. *Do any muscles get damaged more than others?*

The hamstring group of muscles suffers most (they run from your bum down to your knee), because they're 2-joint muscles, connecting to both your pelvis and your knee. With all the stopping, twisting, turning and jumping a player has to do in a game, these muscles come under huge strain

Q. *What's the treatment for this type of injury?*

The best thing for a muscle injury is RICE!

Q. *Rice?? Would that be Rice Pudding, Pilau Rice or even maybe Rice Krispies??? Hmmmmm ..... Rice Krispies!*

None of the above. RICE is an acronym for:

        R - rest

        I - ice

        C - compression

        E - elevation

In other words, stop running, sit down, put a bag of ice on the injury (or frozen peas if you have no ice. Never put ice directly onto your skin - it will stick or can give you an ice burn), strap it up and try to raise it so that gravity helps to keep swelling down. After that it's a question of deep massage, rest and gentle exercise until the muscle has completely healed. Coming back into training or playing too early can damage your career.

Q. *What's the routine when a player goes down injured during a game, and who decides whether he carries on playing or not?*

First I have to wait for the ref's signal before I'm allowed onto the pitch. Once on I'll ask the player what the problem is and assess the injury. I have the final say on whether he stays on or not. Don't forget, I may have treated the player for the same injury in the past, so I'll have a good idea of how bad it is and whether he's going to be able to carry on or not. It may be that he's desperate to stay on, but in the end we both know that if it's going to make the injury worse then it's the wrong thing to do, both short and long term.

Q. *How much of the treatment is in the player's mind, rather than his body?*

There's nearly always a mental side to any injury. Like in all medicine, if you think positively about your injury, and have faith in the treatment, you'll get better more quickly.

[Think about when you turn your ankle in a school match:

Option 1:   Your teacher says, *"That looks pretty painful, you'd better come off."* I bet it felt really sore and you hobbled all the way home, feeling sorry for yourself.

Option 2:   Your teacher says, *"That was a great tackle! I'm not surprised you're hurt because you went in really hard. Try jogging a few steps. It'll hurt for a while, but you're a real tough nut and in a minute or two you won't notice it."* You played the rest of the game, scored a hat-trick (including the winner in the last minute) and were cheered off the pitch.

Maybe that's a bit far-fetched, but you know what I'm getting at. AB]

"Huh! Let your teammates down, would you? Big softy!"

Q. *What's in your bag when you run on the pitch?*

1. Ice and an iced water spray - it helps to numb the painful area, giving instant relief.

2. Tape - for strapping up injured muscles or joints.

3. Gauze and bandages - for treating cuts and grazes.

4. Towel and gloves - it's important to stop the spread of any infection by wearing plastic gloves, and wiping away any blood or sweat from the injured area. Remember, a game can't continue if a player has blood on his body or his kit - surface blood has to be cleaned off and kit changed.

5. Water bottle - to give the injured player a drink. Players have to guard against dehydration, especially in hot weather. Even at school level, when matches are shorter, it's really important that you take plenty of fluid on board.

Q. *What's the worst injury you've seen a player carry on playing with?*

Probably a defender playing on with lacerations (cuts) on the forehead. Even when bandaged up, it must have been murder every time he headed the ball.

Q. *Which T.U.F.C. players stand out as the toughest in the face of injuries?*

In my experience so far I would say probably Kevin Hill and James Sharp.

Q. *Do you have any tips for youngsters to help them avoid injury in a game?*

Plenty of strengthening exercises, particularly of the major leg muscles. The stronger the muscle, the less likely it is to get damaged.

Always warm up and stretch off properly before a game or practice session. Start with a gentle jog to get your heart rate up and increase blood circulation to the muscles, then stretch each of the major leg muscles, holding the stretch for a good long count, rather than 'bouncing' in and out of the stretch position.

Thanks Darren, and good luck for the rest of the season!

* Have you been paying attention in Science lessons?? Why not test your knowledge of muscles and bones with the Sam Skellington challenge on page 88!

January

I have a question for you: Is there anybody out there who really and truly enjoys January? Anyone who, hand on heart, honestly looks forward to it, who wakes up the morning after a New Year's Eve party, gets out of bed, scratches their bum, looks out of the window and exclaims with a cheerful smile: "At last! Thank goodness it's January!" If there is I'd like you to contact me - it'd give me a laugh, cos you're obviously a complete headbanger!

The problem with January is that all the fun times have just gone, and there's nothing on the horizon to look forward to. Even with a boffinish telescope the Easter holidays are a tiny speck in the distance. The mornings are still dark and cold, the evenings are dark and cold, the teachers faces are dark and cold (nothing new there), and if my experience is anything to go by you can also expect the chips you get for school dinner to be dark and cold too.

January is also the month when bad things tend to happen every time you play football. You play in the back garden and your brother whacks the ball from point blank range and it smacks you right on the inside of your thigh, so hard it leaves a crimson ring and the word 'Umbro' back to front, clearly visible every games lesson for the next three weeks

January

Of course your school mates don't find anything at all amusing in this, and certainly wouldn't dream of nicknaming you 'Ballboy' or 'Umbro Dumbo'. Next time out you end up in goal and take the full force of a piledriver right on the end of your thumb, bending it back so it nearly disappears into your elbow. Is there anything more painful??? Answer: yes there is, because when you then get to play out in the street under the lights, you're tripped by the thug next door and go skidding three yards along the road on your bare knees, leaving trails of your own flesh sticking to the tarmac and a raw, bloody, gooey mess where your kneecap used to be. But that's not the most painful bit! No, the real pain comes when you get in, cos your mum takes one look at it and goes off to get the antiseptic from the bathroom cabinet. Soaking a piece of cotton wool in it, she may then try to prepare you for the hellish shock to follow with some totally inadequate warning like: "This may sting a little bit," then Slap! on it goes!

At this point several things happen at once. You get a fierce thudding sensation in the top of your head as it makes contact with the ceiling; the sudden violent upward jerk of your leg boots the cat screeching through the kitchen door; and your neighbours on both sides immediately get on the phone to Social Services to tell them about the torture and brutality that's obviously taking place next door, judging by the crazed screams reverberating through the entire building and all the way down the street.

No, all in all there's not a lot of fun to be had in January. To cap at all, its 31 DAYS LONG! Aaargh!!

Another annoying thing about January is that everybody seems to expect you to make at least one New Year's Resolution. I'm willing to bet that at some time in the past you've been pressured by your parents into making such ridiculous promises such as:

- I'm going to tidy my bedroom and vacuum it every Sunday morning.

- I'm going to eat oranges instead of crisps this year.

- I'm going to get up earlier so that I can make my bed and have a shower every morning.

- I'm going to be nice to my sister and not call her Fishface, Emptyhead or Antbrain.

- I'm going to earn my spending money by cleaning the car every weekend.

- I'm going to practise my times tables for twenty minutes every night until I know them off by heart, and get full marks in all my tests.

What a load of tosh! Research has proved that the average survival time for these 'resolutions' is:

> Girls: Three weeks and two days
>
> Boys: 38.7 minutes

In other words, as everybody knows, you're only making the promise so your parents will get off your back and stop pestering you. They may think they've got you where they want you, but in actual fact you're in a position of power, because if you're smart you only agree to make a resolution yourself if they make one too. You can rest easy because you know from experience that their promises to:

- lose 12 pounds so they can get into that little blue dress they bought two years ago (probably your mum only!)

- redecorate the kitchen and put up new shelves

- go to the gym twice a week

- put some money aside each month so we can go abroad to the sun next Christmas, etc etc

…….. are going to last just as long as yours.

So the conversation around Jan 15th might go:

Dad: *(crossly)* I thought you were going to tidy your room every Sunday? It looks like a bomb site!

You: Sorry Dad. *(innocently)* By the way, were there many people in the gym last night?

Dad: Erm ...... don't change the subject.

You: I only ask because you weren't out for very long, and Billy said he saw you coming out of the Dog and Duck at half seven.

Dad: *(avoiding eye contact)* Er ... was that your mother calling from the kitchen? I'd better go and see what she wants. *(exits rather hurriedly and sheepishly)*

You see how easy it is if you just use a bit of brains?!?

....

As months go, January 2006 might be remembered as one of the most eventful in Torquay United's history. If Channel 4 had bought the rights to film it they could've made a fortune - non-stop drama from start to finish!

The fun (if you can call it that) began on the 2nd of the month, with an away match up at Darlington. Having gone all that way up north, it looked as if we were going to come home with a point when, after trailing 1-2, Alan Connell got on the end of one of Sharpy's legendary long throws to grab what seemed to be a last-minute equaliser. The ref had other ideas however, and awarded a penalty well into stoppage time when the ball struck Sako's hand in a goalmouth scramble. They scored, Sako (a Muslim who spoke hardly any English) supposedly swore at the ref (yeh, right!) and got sent off, and to put the icing on the cake Leroy had to join him when he pulled the half-way flag out and threw it onto the pitch. In his defence he only did what most of our fans felt like doing, except he didn't aim it at the ref! Mind you, I suppose if you're going to lose to a stoppage time penalty it doesn't seem quite so bad when it's scored by someone with such a totally fantastic name as Guylain Ndumbu-Nsungu! The shirt printers up at Darlington must love him!

After such a bitter disappointment, the players had four days to pick themselves up for the visit of Birmingham City in the Cup. Plainmoor was packed to the rafters, the atmosphere was truly memorable, and we played them off the park for most of the game.

Was there ever a better 0-0 draw to watch??? Woodsy rattled the post with a 30-yard thunderbolt, and several times near the end we so nearly nicked a famous and well-deserved victory. Wasn't it great to watch the highlights on Match of the Day, with Lineker, Hansen and Lawro all singing Torquay's praises and saying how brilliant we were! A great day all round. Bring on the replay!

"Come on boss... you've got to look your best for the cameras!"

Next weekend it was back down to reality when we went down 2-3 (again!) at Bury. United dominated for much of the game on a boggy pitch, and went in front through Lockwood, before conceding three goals in a crazy 15-minute spell either side of half-time. Kevin Hill's injury time goal wasn't enough to salvage anything from a very disappointing afternoon.

Tuesday 17th saw a mass exodus from Torquay as fans journeyed to Brum for the cup replay. Just under 2000 made the trip, despite difficulties over ticket sales. Those that made it up to St Andrews saw another tremendous fighting display from the Gulls, only losing to two second half goals. All the players could be proud of their efforts, and the reward for the club was over £100,000 in the bank, thanks to a gate of nearly 25,000 at St Andrews as they slashed ticket prices. We were promised the money would be used to buy new players during the January transfer window - a striker and a midfielder were top priorities, and maybe a defender to replace Adam Lockwood. It was a big blow when Yeovil recalled Lockwood from his loan spell, because he'd started to look the business in the centre of the defence. We couldn't afford to leak more goals if we were to climb up the league.

Another player officially leaving the club (we all knew he wasn't coming back anyway) was Leon Constantine, whose loan deal with Port Vale became a full transfer for £20,000. After paying £70,000 for him it turned out to be a major loss financially, though his poor scoring record suggested that the loss on the pitch might not be quite so great.

The Birmingham matches must have left the players tired but confident. After all, if they could hold their own against Premiership opposition they should be able to cope with Division 2 football. The following week this seemed to be the case, as the boys gave a lesson in passing play to high-flying Grimsby Town. Defensive lapses again took their toll however, and it needed a late point-blank Tony Bedeau header to earn a 2-2 draw.

Never a dull moment at Plainmoor! Disappointingly the crowd was only 2559 - it had been hoped that many of the fans that appeared out of the woodwork for the Birmingham match would carry on turning out for the less glamorous fixtures. Obviously not.

Did I just say 'never a dull moment?' Strictly speaking that continued to be the case, because the Tuesday night match against Rochdale didn't just provide one dull moment, but 89 incredibly dull moments as United were thrashed 3-1. The one bright spot arrived when Sako rose to head home a second half goal to briefly give us hope of a comeback. The display was awful, the team was booed off the pitch at the end, and it was plain that something was seriously wrong. It was no real surprise when the news was announced the next day that after talks with Mike Bateson, Leroy and the club had agreed to part company.

The Herald Express paid tribute to a manager who had earned the respect of the fans for a style of football not often seen in the lower leagues. The response of fans was mixed - appreciation of the belief in passing over muscle, but realisation of the fact that it simply wasn't getting the results needed to keep the club in the Football League. A great shame. Farewell and good luck Leroy!

Within two days John Cornforth had been appointed as new caretaker manager. He arrived following mixed spells at Exeter and Newport, but whatever he said to the players obviously worked, because his first two games in charge resulted in a 1-0 away win at Shrewsbury, then a vital 1-1 draw at bottom club Stockport County.

Leroy's sudden departure left Corny with only five days to make new signings before the transfer window closed, an impossible situation for a new caretaker manager. The money from the cup run remained in the bank, and we had to be content with two loan deals - John McCombe, a centre half on a one-month deal from Huddersfield, and Les Afful, a forward signed for three months from Exeter. To add some stability to the squad, Sako and Darren Garner were taken off the transfer list. Thank goodness Mike Bateson was able to reject last-minute offers for both Sako and Jo Kuffour - the last few days had shown a light at the end of the tunnel: the weeks ahead would need everyone to stick together and fight as one for the club's survival.

January Quotes:

"Premier League? You're havin' a laugh!"
Fans taunt outplayed Birmingham City during FA Cup clash.

" .... "
Leroy is left speechless after his last match in charge against Rochdale.

"Yesterday I was out walking the dog, today I'm back doing what I love most and know best, being in charge of a football team, and I'm relishing the challenge."
John Cornforth, on being appointed Caretaker Manager.

"We were terrific for most of the game. But it's not rocket science to ask players to concentrate for 90 minutes to win a game."
Corny is disappointed following dropped points against Grimsby.

January Stats

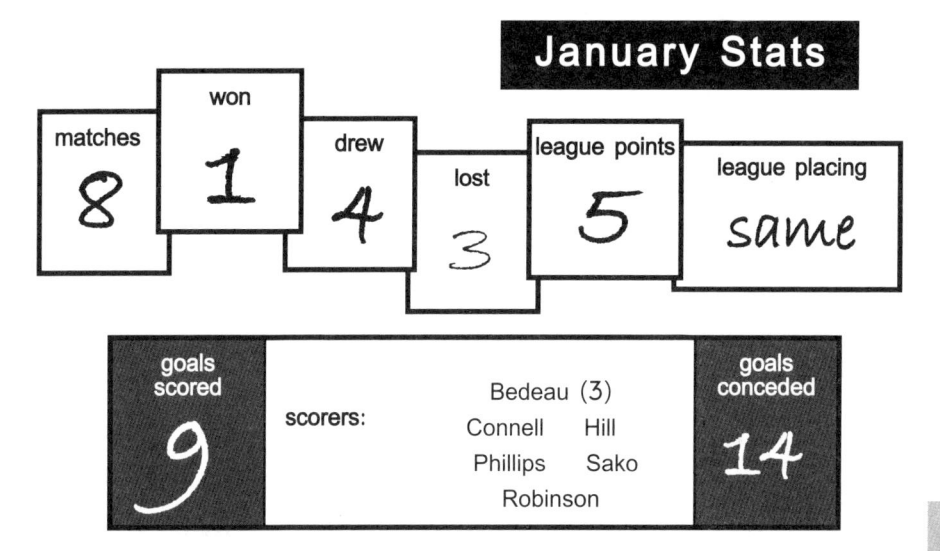

matches	8
won	1
drew	4
lost	3
league points	5
league placing	same

goals scored	scorers:		goals conceded
9	Bedeau (3) Connell Hill Phillips Sako Robinson		14

players used	17
average match time in possession of ball	50%

yellow cards	red cards
7	2

fouls	by United	by opponents
	94	94

goal attempts	by United	by opponents
	69	94

total attendance	total miles travelled
49,315	2,605
Ave: 6,164	

Table at end of January

	P	W	D	L	F	A	GD	Pts
Wycombe W.	30	13	15	2	55	34	21	54
Carlisle Utd	30	15	6	9	49	32	17	51
Grimsby Town	30	15	6	9	46	29	17	51
Northampton	30	12	14	4	43	25	18	50
Leyton Orient	29	14	8	7	48	39	9	50
Darlington	30	11	11	8	42	32	10	44
Peterborough	30	11	10	9	39	29	10	43
Cheltenham	29	11	10	8	38	36	2	43
Notts County	30	11	10	9	34	39	-5	43
Bristol Rovers	30	12	6	12	41	48	-7	42
Boston United	30	9	13	8	36	38	-2	40
Lincoln City	30	8	15	7	36	34	2	39
Wrexham	28	10	8	10	40	32	8	38
Rochdale	29	11	5	13	48	47	1	38
Shrewsbury	30	9	10	11	35	36	-1	37
Chester City	29	9	9	10	41	39	2	36
Macclesfield	30	8	12	10	41	48	-7	36
Oxford United	30	8	10	12	29	39	-10	34
Mansfield T.	30	8	8	14	39	47	-8	32
Barnet	29	7	11	11	28	38	-10	32
Bury	27	8	6	13	30	41	-11	30
Torquay Utd	**30**	**6**	**10**	**14**	**37**	**54**	**-17**	**28**
Stockport C.	29	4	15	10	35	56	-21	27
Rushden/D.	29	6	8	15	30	48	-18	26

January

Any Fizzy O! will tell you how important it is to have full knowledge of the bones and muscles that make up the human body.

Your challenge, should you choose to accept it, is to take the names from the box and write them in the spaces.

O1! WHO NICKED ME CLOTHES

Sam Skellington

1. _____
2. _____
3. _____
4. _____
5. _____
6. _____
7. _____
8. _____
9. _____
10. _____
11. _____
12. _____
13. _____
14. _____

HAMSTRING
PELVIS
PATELLA
RIBS
CRANIUM
QUADRICEPS
FIBULA
VERTEBRA
METATARSALS
COLLAR BONE
ACHILLES TENDON
TIBIA
CALF
FEMUR

CAN WE HAVE OUR BALL BACK PLEASE..

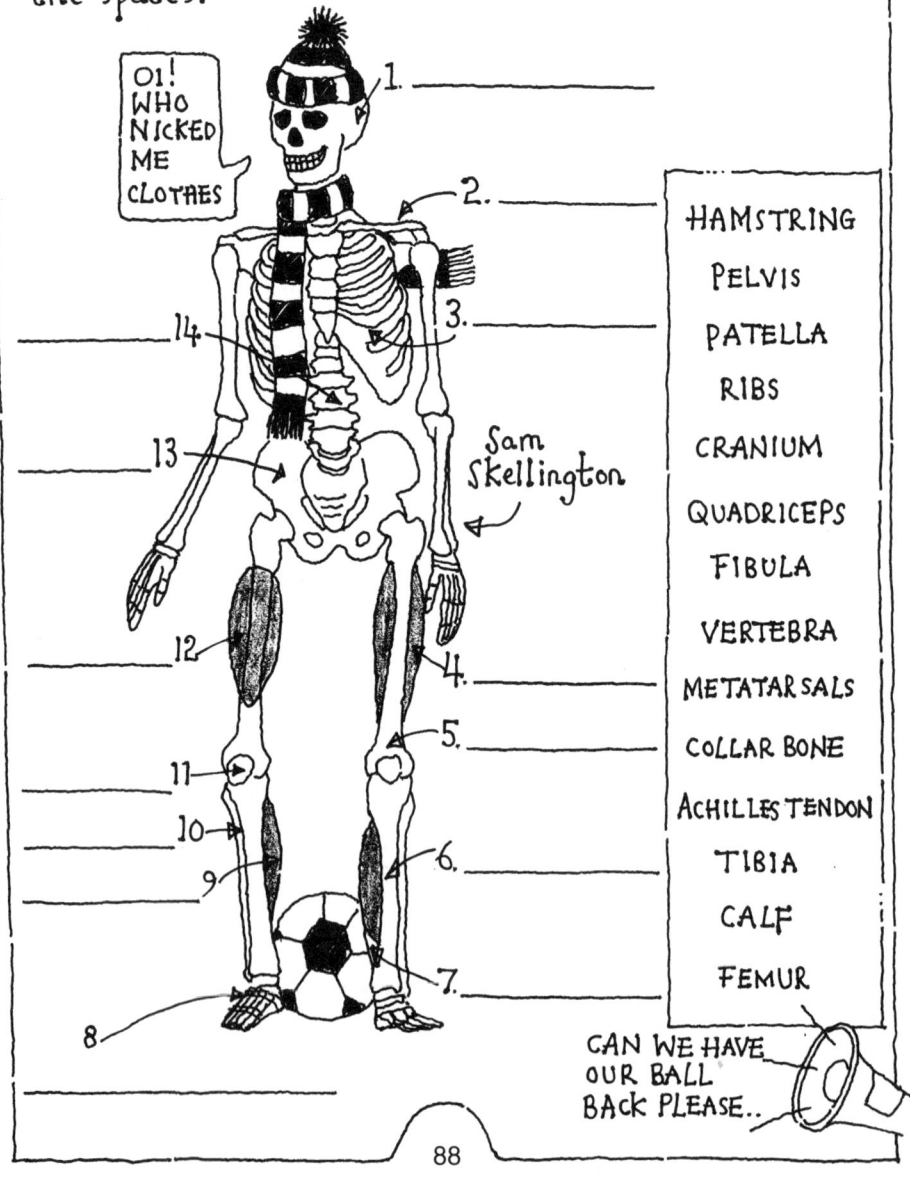

88

Players who don't ask for a transfer are often entitled to 5% of any transfer fee. Some well-travelled players could almost make a living from their moves without kicking a ball in anger!

CAN YOU WORK OUT HOW MUCH THE PLAYERS WOULD GET FROM THE TRANSFER DEALS:

AB's TIP!

There are various ways to find 5% of a number without a calculator:

- You can ÷ by 100 then × by 5.
- You can ÷ it by 20.
- The easiest way is to ÷ by 10 and then halve it!

and his collection of 'Spice Girls' CDs!

Player	From	To	Fee	5%
Beckham	Real	Chelsea	£35 m	
Ronaldo	Man Utd	Milan	£12 m	
Villis	Torquay	Arsenal	£400,000	
Lampard	Chelsea	Barcelona	£32 m	
Shufflebottom	Barton	Hele	£8,000	
Ronaldinho	Barcelona	Torquay	£57 m	

and a kebab from the local chippy!

Billy and his mates follow the Gulls everywhere they go. Last week they went up to Bristol Rovers to watch yet another United away win.

At half time they went to Peckish Percy's Pasty Bar for some grub. Here's the menu:

Peckish Percy's
pasty Bar

that's yummy

Cornish Pasty	£1.40	Super Burger	£1.30
Steak Pasty	£1.50	Chips	80p
Curry Pasty	£1.35	Mushy Peas	70p
Special Pasty	£1.60	Crisps	45p
Beef Pie	£1.20	Tea	65p
Chicken Pie	£1.15	Coffee	85p
Pizza slice	90p	Bovril	60p
Jumbo Hot Dog	£1.25	Soft Drinks	55p

really huge...

and that...

these come with a lid so you don't spill it!

Please place all your rubbish in the bins provided around the grounds. Thank you!

menu!

Billy got a pasty, mushy peas and tea. It cost him £2.85. Which pasty did he get?

Bobby bought a pizza slice, two packets of crisps and a Bovril. How much did it cost him?

Berty's bill came to £2.80. He ate chicken pie and chips, but...... which drink did he throw all over his shirt when Mickey Evans scored just after half time?

Barry spent £2.40 on a Bovril and some food. What did he have to eat?

WARNING

This one's a bit complicated! Betty was buying for herself and her 3 children. She had a Beef Pie, while two of her kids had hot dogs and the other had a burger. They got two portions of chips to share between them. Betty had a nice cup of tea and each of the kids had a soft drink. They bought crisps for the second half and also for the long drive home. If the cost altogether was £12.05, how many packets of crisps did they buy?

MUMMY I FEEL SICK...

There's a well known story about a newspaper reporter who once asked a famous player for an interview after a match. The player replied aggressively that he'd never speak to the reporter again after what he'd written about him following the last match. Puzzled, the reporter went away, looked up the match report and saw that he'd described the player's performance as 'ubiquitous'.

Was the player right to be angry? (look it up!!)

Here are some other words that might well crop up in a newspaper or magazine to describe a player or his performance. Imagine you're the player in question.

Put a tick against the ones you'd treat as a compliment, and a cross against those you'd be unhappy with:

| flamboyant | ☐ | execrable | ☐ | dynamic | ☐ |
| ingenious | ☐ | diffident | ☐ | indefatigable | ☐ |

United played Liverpool in an FA Cup replay, starting at 7.30. There were 3 minutes added at the end of each half, and at the final whistle the score was 2-2. There was a 5-minute break before two 15-minute periods of extra time, with 2 minutes to change over in between periods. After all that it was still a draw, so penalties had to be taken. Sorting out the takers caused a delay of 8 minutes, and then the penalties took 13 minutes before Steve Woods scored the winning spot kick.

What time did the game finally end?

new scarf for next season!

What's that on the 24 hour clock? ☐

knit one, pearl one.....

YOU ANY GOOD WITH A NATLESS?

Use one to match up these clubs with the towns marked on the map. Write the letter next to the clubs name. (Yes, I know there's one missing, you'll just have to work it out won't you!)

.... Hartlepool United   .... Chester City
.... Stockport County   .... Lincoln City
.... Shrewsbury Town   .... Bristol Rovers
.... Accrington Stanley   .... Walsall
.... Wycombe Wanderers   ....?

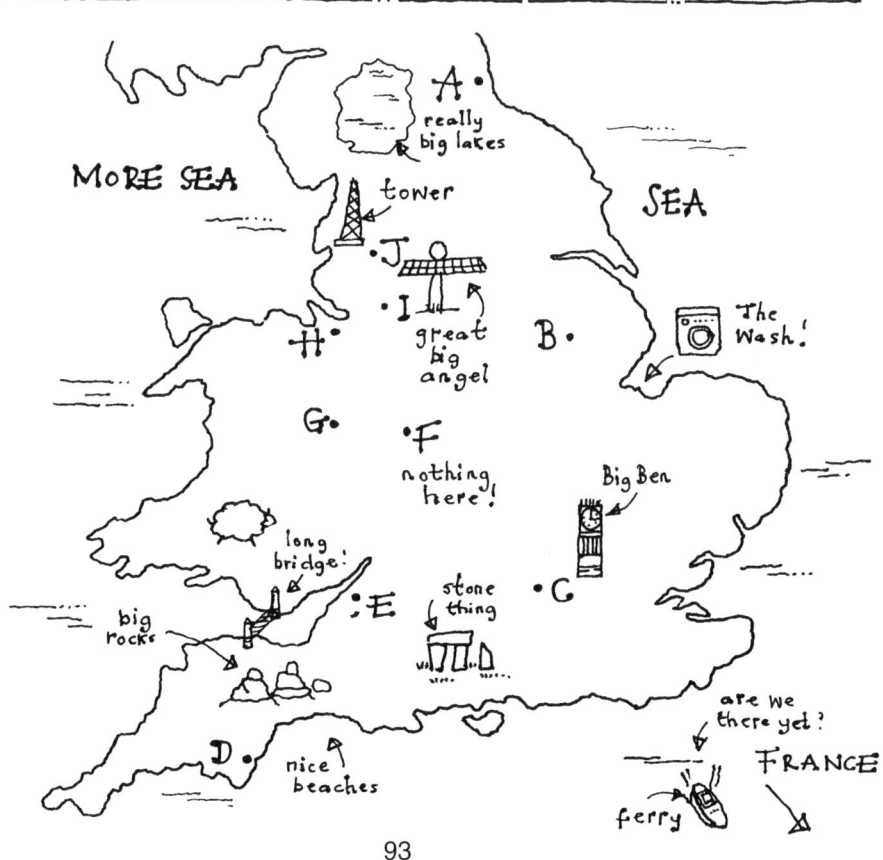

MEANWHILE IN THE GYM.....

To increase muscle bulk, weight trainers will usually use a heavy weight and do fewer repetitions (reps) in each set. Often with each set they will reduce the number of reps as the muscles tire. Lee Thorpe and Mickey Evans were doing bench presses together.

LEE USED A 45 kg WEIGHT AND DID SETS OF 6, 5 AND 4 PRESSES.

MICKEY USED A 35 kg WEIGHT BUT DID MORE REPS, 8, 7 AND 6.

Who lifted more weight, and how much more?

little lifty thing

TOTAL

Matt Villis decided to work on muscle tone rather than bulk, so he used a lighter weight but did more repetitions. He did 4 sets of 14, 12, 10 and 8 reps, and lifted a total of 660 kg

WHAT WEIGHT WAS HE USING??

TOTAL

After 3 weeks weight training, Mattie Hewlett found that his weight had gone up from 74.60 kg to 76.25 kg. This is to be expected, as gaining muscle means gaining weight.

HOW MANY GRAMS HAD HIS WEIGHT RISEN BY?

TOTAL

February

Let's hear it for February! Hip hip! .... Come on, you can do better than that! Hip hip! .... All right, I give in. Boring. Tedious. Dark. Cold. Windy. Miserable. Can you think of any more words to describe February? (and what's that extra 'r' all about??? Nobody ever says it! Be honest, do you know anyone who actually says it Feb-roo-ary? I thought not. It's Feb-u-ary, so let's cut all the nonsense and do away with that 'r'. You know it makes sense!)

No, Febuary (from now on that's how I'm going to spell it, as my own personal protest against silly English spelling. Yes, I know I'm acting like a big baby, but there you go) really needs something to spice it up. It needs an event, a happening, a big story. Something to make it come alive and stick in the memory.

Let's have a search through our imaginary news archive and see what we can come up with

Torbay Tribune

Friday 18th February 2007

Mystery Bug Wipes Out Teachers!!!

The mystery illness that has struck down more than 3500 teaching staff nationwide in the last two weeks has spread to the South West. Hospitals have reported a dramatic increase in the number of teachers being admitted, and are hard pressed to cope with the situation. Doris Bimp, senior registrar at Torquay Hospital For The Pretty Poorly, explained: *"If this goes on we're going to run out of beds within the next forty eight minutes. We'll have them lying in the corridors, under the stairs, in the gardener's shed, even in the car park ...... though as they're only teachers I don't suppose it matters really."*

We asked an international expert on teacher-related diseases, Doctor Heinrich Gershplatt, to try to explain the reasons behind the sudden spread of the disease, and to identify the common symptoms.

"Vell, you haff to understand that teachers are a strange breed of humanoid life form. They tend to stick together in tight packs, sheltering in their shtaff rooms. Under these circumstances any infection vill spread like the vildfire. It only needs one teecher to trink coffee from an infected teecher's mug and before you can say Shack Robinson it vill be all around the shkool.

Bug-eyed

As teachers like to spend as much time as possible in meetings out of the shkool rather than in the classrooms, clearly the bug vill be all over the town like a rash in the plink of an eye. As for the symptoms, children need to vatch their teecher closely for any of the following tell-tale signs:

- *frothing at the mouth*
- *going all bug-eyed*
- *shcreaming a lot*
- *the face going extremely red, so that it looks as if you could fry an egg on it*
- *dramatic mood swings*
- *muttering and cursing under the breath a crate deal.*

Boils

If you see any or all of these signs in your teacher please call a doctor immediately, as they indicate that the second stage of the illness is about to begin. This is vere things get really nasty, as the teacher vill come out in crate purple boils the size of saucers, the shkin vill start to turn a very sickly shade of green and the tongue vill swell right up and stick right out of the mouth, giving them the appearance of some giant slimy lizard in a cheap suit."

Bag over head

Schools across the region are expected to close for at least three weeks, while all teachers have been strictly ordered to remain in their homes with a bag over their head to prevent the spread of the disease to normal people.

A Tale Of Three Bosses

Leroy Rosenior (above) was praised for his pure football style, but left in January following a series of disappointing performances by his team.

John Cornforth (right) took over, but was in the hot seat for less than two months as Chairman Mike Bateson searched for the winning formula and league survival.

Finally *Ian Atkins* (below) was given the task of guiding the Gulls to safety. Six matches later that miracle was achieved on the back of five wins and a draw.

Photos: Colin Bratcher

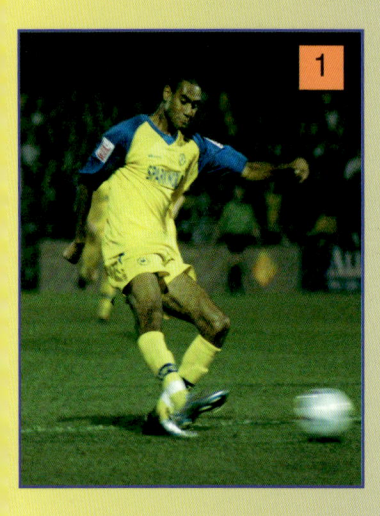

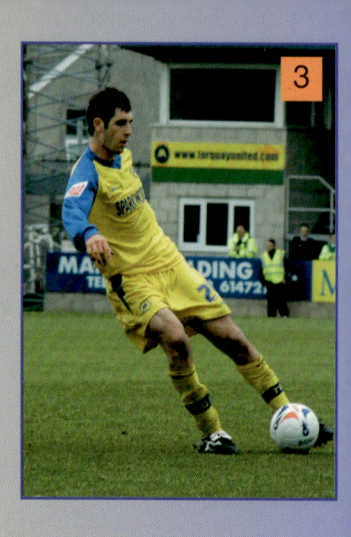

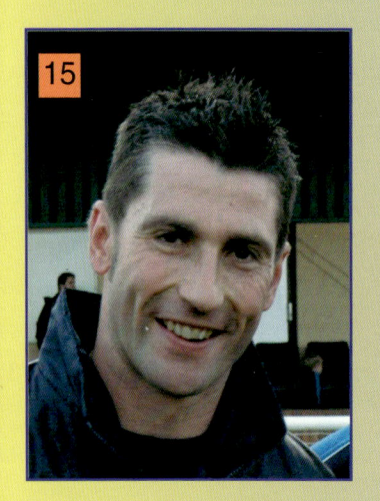

TEST YOUR MEMORY!

On this double page are 15 players who played their part at United last season (some more than others), but are no longer at the club.

How many can you name?

(first *and* second names, please)

Answers p 159

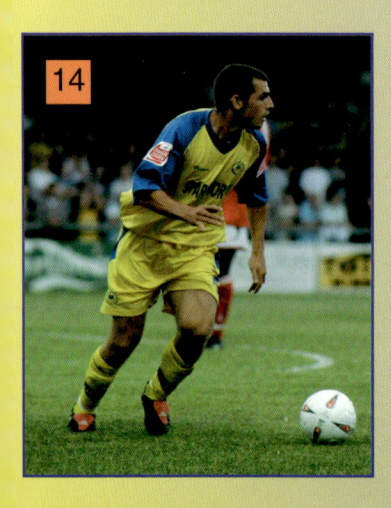

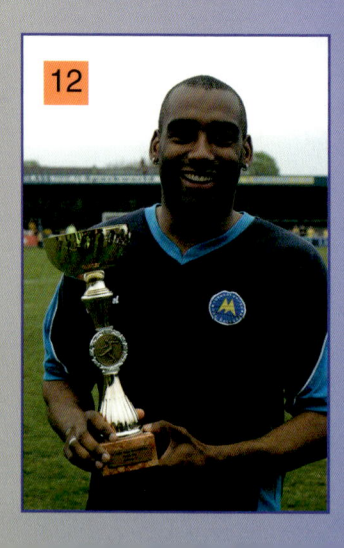

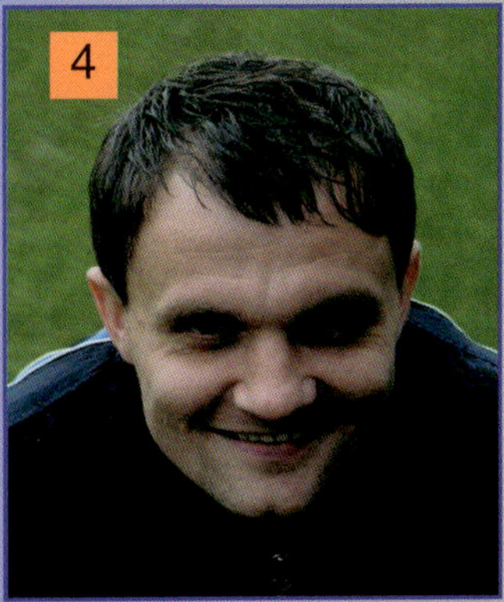
4

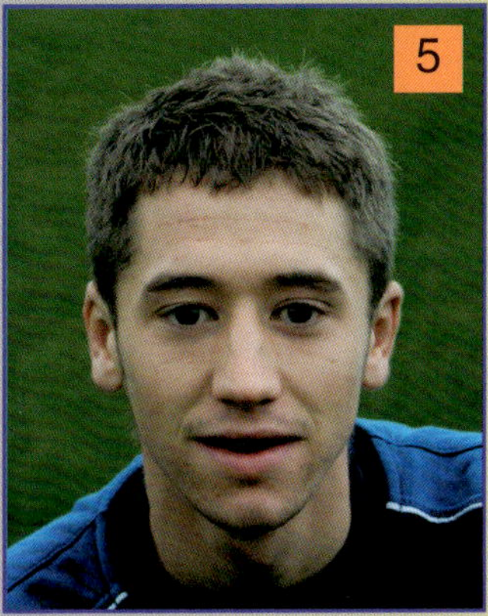
5

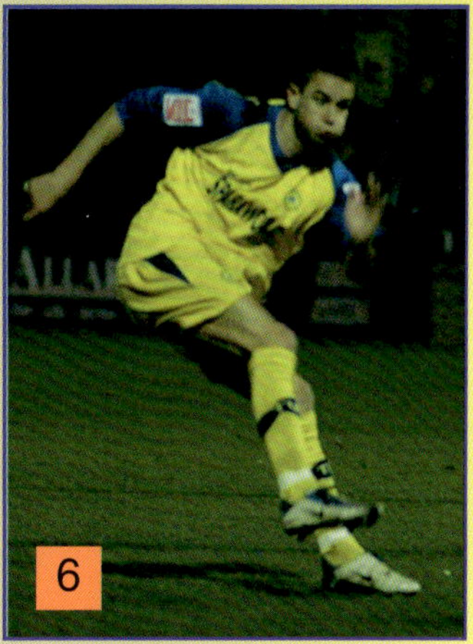
6

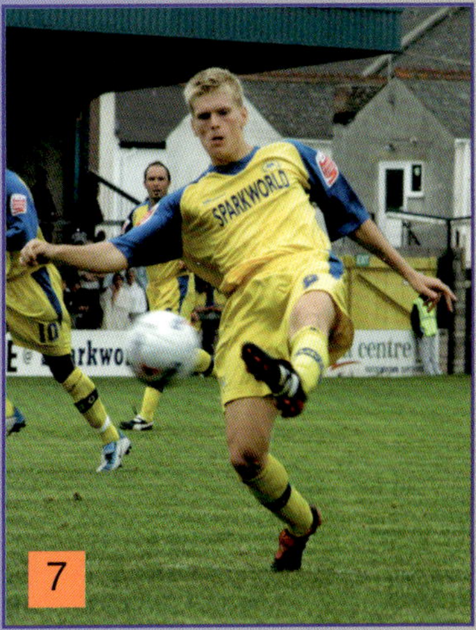
SPARKWORLD
7

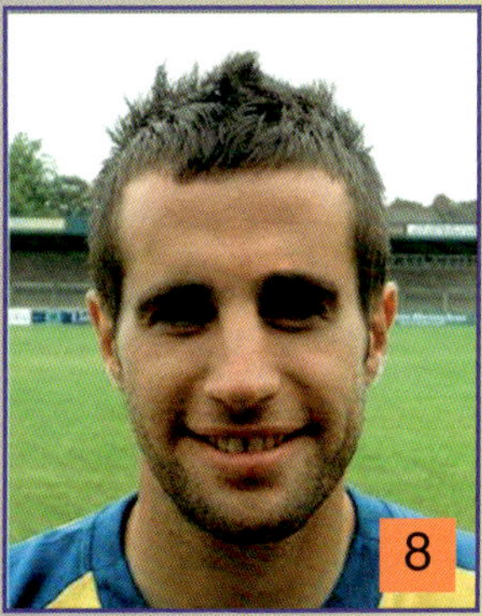
8

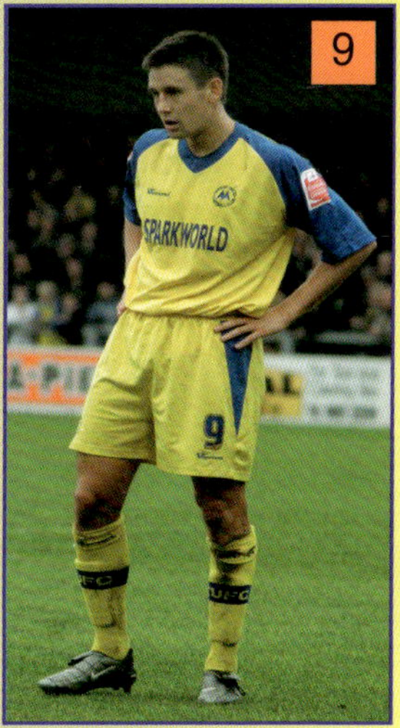
9
SPARKWORLD

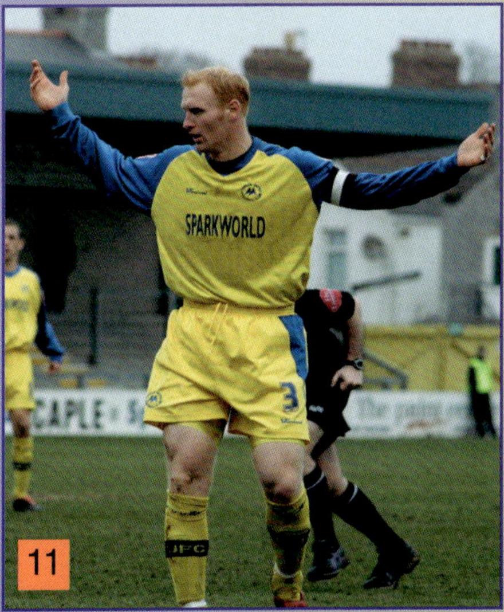
SPARKWORLD
11

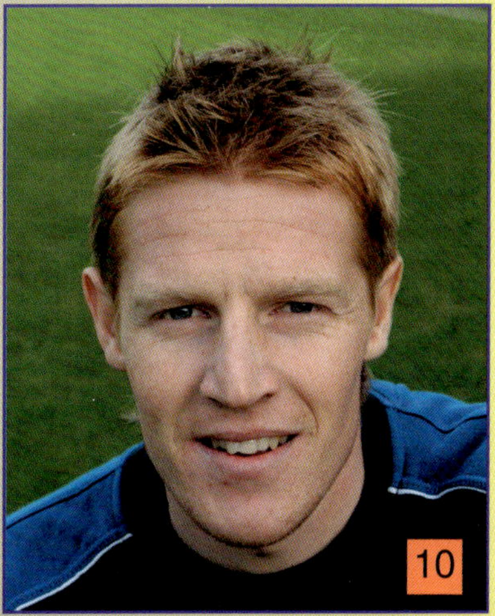
10

The magic of the Cup: Buster Phillips displays perfect balance as he runs rings round the Birmingham City defence. Steve Bruce (inset) admitted his team were lucky to escape with a draw.

Fans climb the floodlights to get a view of the United v Spurs FA Cup clash at Plainmoor in 1965. Ok until you find you need a wee .... "Look out below!!!"

United 2
Orient 0
Feb 4th 2006

(the day the lights went out)

"Right lads, it's too dark for football so we're going to play hide-and-seek. Buster, you're on. Count to 500 in 5s, and no peeping. And no hiding in Boots And Laces!"

"Come on ref, it's way past our bedtime!"

"Don't worry lads. Finish the game, then I'll make you a nice cup of cocoa, tuck you in and read you a story."

Later, searchlights are used to try to track down the Orient players and foil their cunning plan to escape under cover of darkness.

CHARGE OF THE LIGHT BRIGADE

Monday's Herald Express headline.

Lee Thorpe's spectacular bicycle kick opened the scoring and set the tone for the evening (above).

He added a headed second before Jo Kuffour fired a third (left) and was immediately engulfed by his team mates (below).

ONE CRAZY NIGHT IN APRIL!

United 4   Stockport County 0

Danny Hollands killed off all thoughts of a fightback when he coolly lobbed a fourth goal just after half-time (above).

Unable to cope with the acute embarrassment of a heavy defeat, a member of the NNS (Northern Nutters Society) tried to get the game abandoned by swinging on the crossbar after 12 pasties. His desperate and rather childish stunt ended in failure, and he was led way to have his stomach pumped.

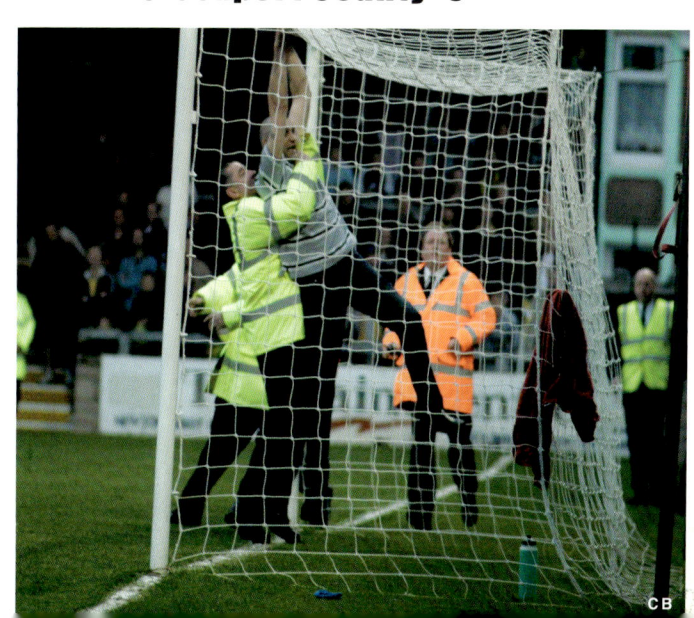

Safe! Joyous fans flood the Plainmoor pitch in celebration after the last match against Boston in May.

STRIP!

Here are 5 United kits from the past.
Can you match up the kits with these seasons???

1935   1957   1975   1992   1996   2004

(answers p159)

A

B

C

D

E

F

Babbacombe Bugle

Friday 13th February 2007

FREAK WEATHER SET TO CONTINUE

By our South West correspondent.

There appears to be no end in sight to the freak weather pattern that has seen schools in Torbay closed for the third consecutive week. Scientists are at a loss to explain why heavy localised snowfalls have occurred on each of the last three Sunday nights, continuing during the week until miraculously clearing on Friday afternoon, giving way to clear, sunny weekends.

While children have been kept away from school for safety reasons, teaching staff have been required to attend each day as usual for training, preparation, gossip and some serious coffee drinking purposes.

Poisoned

Spokesperson Fred Grone commented: *"While it's obviously disappointing not to have the little pests - sorry, children around the place, it has given us the chance to have some fantastic meetings, some lasting a full five hours. The only downside is the caffeine poisoning that has struck down three of our staff already."*

Kids meanwhile have been understandably delighted with this turn of events. Weekdays spent lazing at home or having snowball fights in the street have been followed by weekends of sport, play and fun annoying parents. Only a tiny minority have expressed any dismay about not being able to attend school, and these have generally been silenced by a hail of snowballs or a heap of slush crammed down the back of their shirt. *"It's been great to have this extra unexpected holiday,"* said one Paignton boy. *"And with all this additional training they're getting, just think how clever our teachers will be by the time we eventually get back to school!"*

February

Aaaah, if only dreams really did come true!!!

As for happenings at the club, Febuary certainly started dramatically. As expected, John Cornforth was announced as the new manager on Friday

3rd, and the very next day United climbed out of the bottom three for the first time since October 7th following a 2-0 win over high-flying Leyton Orient. After a goalless first half Buster Phillips's cross shot put us one up seconds after the restart, while half the crowd were still either in the toilet or the pasty queue. Tony Bedeau then showed that goal-scoring had become so easy he needed a new challenge - he decided to lie down before knocking the ball over the line! With Matt Villis playing a blinder in defence Torquay were in total control and the game seemed to be drifting towards a straightforward finish when suddenly, with only seven minutes to go........

the lights went out.

This didn't appear at first to be any problem, as the light was obviously perfectly good enough to finish the game. According to referee Andy Penn, he was forced to stop the game for safety reasons (what, players being blinded by the sun???). Losing 0-2, the Orient manager and players were off like a shot,

"D'you think they're trying to make a point?"

heading for the tunnel. Mr Penn called them back, and there then followed ten minutes or so of chit chat while we waited for the lights to go back on. They didn't. Off went the players, and we were left in the dark, wondering how life could be so cruel. Help was at hand, however, in the form of Kim Prestwood and Mark Vickary, local electricians who between them managed to get a few of the lights back on. Out came the players again, very reluctantly in Orient's case, and to huge cheers from the crowd the game restarted. The daft thing was that it was now much darker than it had been when they all went off in the first place! There was no more drama, we got our three points and Kim and Mark made it on to the front page of Monday's Herald Express.

With two wins and a draw in their first three games under Corny the Gulls travelled up to Lincoln hoping to put together a run which would finally pull them away from the threat of relegation. Corny's policy of setting up reserve games to keep everybody match-sharp was paying off, fitness and confidence seemed to be on the up, clubs around them were struggling - surely this was the chance to put some distance between us and the trapdoor.

As had been the case all season, however, that string of good results just didn't happen. A 0-2 defeat at Lincoln, courtesy of a deflection and a late clincher, once again left us questioning if we really were good enough to stay up. One of the marks of a good team is consistency, the ability to grind out wins or draws even when not at your best. While our results were slowly improving, not once so far had we been able to win two matches on the trot. That's always going to put a team under pressure.

A series of poor results had seen Bury dragged down into the relegation battle, and so the Tuesday night meeting at Plainmoor had added importance for both clubs. A win was vital. Kevin Hill became only the fifth person to play 400 games for the club and was rightly given a standing ovation. Lee Thorpe, newly arrived on loan from Swansea, made his debut at centre forward. Unfortunately the weather decided to get in the way. A howling gale blew down the pitch, joined by driving rain, making any kind of constructive football impossible. Bury just about had the better of a bitterly disappointing game, the goalies between them had only seven saves to make, and it's probably true to say that for most fans the major highlight was the pasty and Bovril at half time.

An even game away at Northampton was decided by a late goal (not for us, I'm afraid), and when in-form Mansfield arrived in town we were treated once again to typical Torbay Febuary weather. In a carbon copy of the Bury game United played against the hurricane in the first half, going in 0-1 down after an almighty goalmouth scramble resulted in probably the ugliest goal seen at Plainmoor all season. With the wind at their backs in the second half United rained shots down on the Mansfield goal, but as so often during the season the ball just wouldn't go in, seeming to highlight the need for an out-and-out goalscorer in the team. To rub salt into the wounds the visitors broke upfield near the end to claim a second goal.

Rushden and Diamonds' three points from a win against Macclesfield bounced them back above United, leaving us at the bottom of the pile once more, a situation made all the worse by the fact that we'd played more games than nearly all of the clubs above us. Things were indeed getting rather serious. We weren't done for yet, but the Fat Lady had cleared her throat and was beginning to do her warm-up exercises.

February Quotes:

"There are massive rewards for players if they want them; you don't have to be in the Premiership now to be a wealthy man, and they've got that chance that thousands and thousands of kids would just love. It's all about hard work."

"[some players] who've played every game and perhaps had a cushy ride may see that coming to an end. I've never been bothered what players think of me. As long as they perform they'll stay in the team. Simple."
John Cornforth makes his feelings clear regarding fitness and attitude.

"When I first walked in the door, I said I couldn't understand why this squad of players was down in this position. I've seen why today. I think we carried about five or six [of them]."
Corny pulls no punches after the Mansfield game.

February Stats

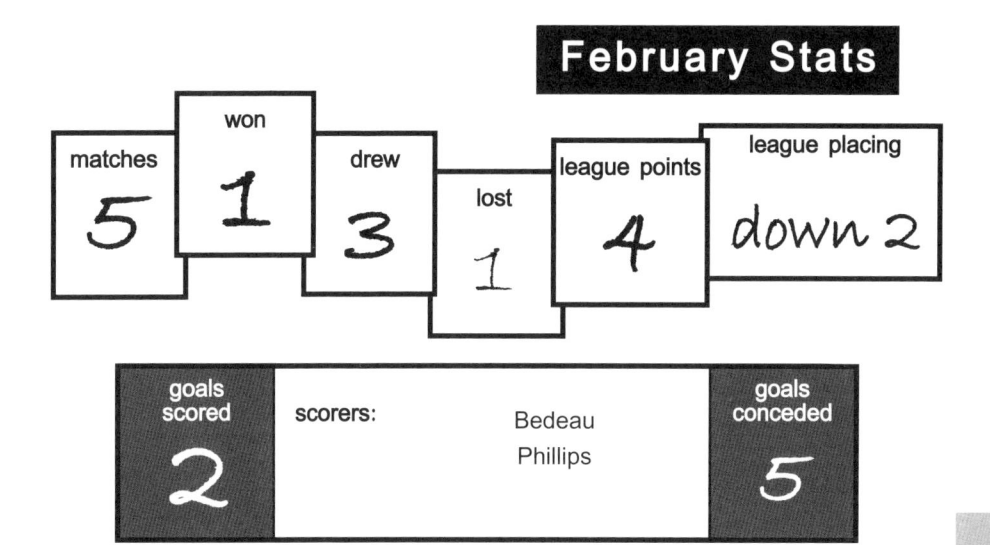

- matches: 5
- won: 1
- drew: 3
- lost: 1
- league points: 4
- league placing: down 2

- goals scored: 2
- scorers: Bedeau, Phillips
- goals conceded: 5

- players used: 18
- average match time in possession of ball: 49%

- yellow cards: 5
- red cards: 0

- fouls by United: 54
- fouls by opponents: 75
- goal attempts by United: 54
- goal attempts by opponents: 52

- total attendance: 17,400
- total miles travelled: 984
- Ave: 3,480

Table at end of February

	P	W	D	L	F	A	GD	Pts
Carlisle Utd	35	18	8	9	63	35	28	62
Wycombe W.	35	15	17	3	62	41	21	62
Northampton	35	15	15	5	49	29	20	60
Grimsby Town	34	18	6	10	50	31	19	60
Leyton Orient	35	16	11	8	52	42	10	59
Peterborough	35	14	10	11	46	35	11	52
Lincoln City	35	12	16	7	47	40	7	51
Cheltenham	34	13	12	9	44	40	4	51
Darlington	35	11	13	11	44	37	7	46
Wrexham	32	12	9	11	46	35	11	45
Boston United	34	10	15	9	38	40	-2	45
Shrewsbury	35	11	11	13	40	41	-1	44
Notts County	35	11	10	14	37	47	-10	43
Bristol Rovers	35	14	8	13	47	53	-6	42
Rochdale	33	11	8	14	51	53	-2	41
Mansfield T.	35	10	11	14	48	53	-5	41
Macclesfield	34	8	15	11	44	52	-8	39
Oxford United	34	8	13	13	33	44	-11	37
Bury	33	9	10	14	33	44	-11	37
Barnet	34	8	13	13	32	43	-11	37
Chester City	33	9	9	15	42	49	-7	36
Stockport C.	34	6	16	12	44	63	-19	34
Rushden/D.	35	8	9	18	33	58	-25	33
Torquay Utd	**35**	**7**	**11**	**17**	**39**	**59**	**-20**	**32**

March

With games beginning to run out and United still rooted to the bottom of the league, results were desperately needed. So far we'd been lucky – when we had a bad spell the clubs around us did too. We could already have found ourselves in a hopeless situation, tailed off with only the prospect of thrashing Exeter in the Conference next season to look forward to. As it was, we were still very much in touch. But we needed wins!

A poor run of results had seen Chester City sucked down into the relegation zone, and so our first game of the month up there would be one of many '6-pointers' before the season was out. Steven Reed, on loan from Yeovil, was set to make his debut in the problem left-back slot - Brian McGlinchey, the Northern Ireland Under-21 international, had that month been forced to give up his battle against a persistent back injury and retire from the game. Anthony Lloyd had done a decent job filling in, but whereas he was right-footed Reed was a natural left-footer, an advantage when swinging those crosses in. Buster Phillips was still out, but Lee Thorpe returned to action after a one-match ban, and so with their ears still ringing from their blasting after the Mansfield game, the team set off up the M5 in determined mood.

Unlike when you go on holiday, I don't suppose they had to stop off at Exeter services to have a wee/buy sweets/eat sweets/buy fizzy drink/play on machines/run around like a mad animal on grass/throw up on grass/buy more sweets/have another wee/buy fizzy drink for the car (do cars even *like* fizzy drinks?)/find car after 10 mins searching round car park/get in car/decide you need another wee .....etc etc. No, they probably didn't stop at Exeter services, although they might as well have done, because they hadn't even got out of Devon when a phone call confirmed that heavy snow had made the Chester pitch unplayable and they'd have to turn round and come home again (no, I don't know if they stopped to buy sweets on the way back). This was a real pain, because it meant a wasted day with no training. Plenty of other games were called off due to the snow, but most of those decisions had been made on the Friday, allowing teams to stay at home and do some training instead. Corny was not best pleased.

The game was rescheduled for the Tuesday night, and though United returned with a point, the general view was that it was two points dropped rather than one gained. In front of their lowest league crowd of the season (only 1806) Kevin Hill's drive put United into a first-half lead, and at half-time they were looking comfortable. The game turned when Thorpe was sent off for allegedly head-butting Chester's Ben Davies. The video showed that some contact was made, but it hardly merited Davies' WWF performance, collapsing as if he'd been shot by a sniper. In the end the Gulls were lucky to come away with a draw, and the red card meant that Thorpe would have a three-game break to reflect on his hot-headedness (literally).

The following week saw yet more new arrivals through the turnstiles at Plainmoor. 20-year-old Danny Hollands was beamed up from Chelsea reserves and dropped straight into the centre of Torquay's midfield. He soon looked as though he'd been playing there all his life – talk about being comfortable on the ball, he looked as if he had time to make a phone call, write a postcard, scratch his bum and have a cup of tea before choosing who to pass to.

Then on the Friday it was announced that Ian Atkins had been given the job of 'football advisor' (whatever that's supposed to mean. Isn't that the manager's job?). Corny was very polite and made all the right comments about how Ian's experience would be a great help, and how much he was looking forward to working with him, but he must have been wondering what was going on. After all, Atkins had applied for the manager's job when Corny was appointed (and when Leroy was appointed too).

However, both Atkins and Hollands seemed to have an immediate effect on the team, who put in a great performance to beat Peterborough 1-0 and lift the club off the bottom once again. Tony Bedeau got the only goal with a volley into the bottom corner, but it was the all-round display that was most encouraging. Hollands brought culture and invention to the midfield and Matt Villis was outstanding in a solid defence that also saw the return of captain Craig Taylor. Strange as it may seem, Bedeau's goal was the only goal seen at Plainmoor during the whole of March. Contrast that with the heady days of December, when home fans were treated to 19 goals, 10 of them scored by United! Thankfully a decent crowd was there to witness the win, despite a call from some 'supporters' to boycott the game and go and watch Dawlish Town instead. To their great credit Dawlish wanted no part in this, suggesting any true fans should be getting behind their team during difficult times, not making things worse.

With a win under their belts the team travelled up to promotion-chasing Wycombe Wanderers full of confidence. After all, they had nothing to lose. As Corny said before the match: *"These are the games you love to be a part of, when everybody in the country doesn't expect you to win."* So what did we go and do? We only won, that's what! A crowd of over 7,000 watched the game, easily the highest of the season so far for a Torquay match. Tony Bedeau again got the goal that brought home the three points, but it was a fantastic work rate, a

> **Joke!**
>
> **Footballer**: Yesss!!!
> **Wife**: What's that babes?
> **Footballer**: I've finished my jigsaw, and it only took me 8 months and 12 days!
> **Wife**: Is that good?
> **Footballer**: Good?? It's brilliant! It says 4 - 6 years on the box!

they-shalt-not-pass approach from the whole team and just a smidgen of luck that gave us the win. United were under the cosh for much of the game, especially towards the end, and only spectacular goal-line blocks from Marriott and Woods saved the day. For the first time all season United had put together two consecutive wins, and were now up to 21st - only the second time since the season's opening day that they'd been so high! Bedeau's goals earned him the Division 2 Player of the Month award. You may think that's a bit much for only two goals, but apparently these days they judge these things on how important the goals are, and as both resulted in vital wins he got the nod.

A win at home to struggling Stockport would surely put the seal on a great month and ease our relegation fears once and for all. That sounds familiar …… ah yes, we said the same thing in December when we were due to play Stockport away after a great home performance against Wycombe. That time the freezing weather got in the way and the game was postponed. Funny how life seems to repeat itself, isn't it? This time two days of torrential rain, combined with gale-force winds, meant that the Plainmoor pitch looked more like Plainmoor Swimming Pool next door. The ref decided that it would only be fit for a game between the ducks, the seagulls, children with water wings and Noah. Chairman Mike Bateson reckoned this latest postponement would cost the club £7000 – firstly we would have to pay for Stockport's travel and accommodation for the rescheduled match. Secondly, this would have to be an evening kick-off, meaning fewer away fans would be able to travel down. What a pest!

The month did finish with some kind of good news, however, when Leroy was taken onto the coaching staff at Shrewsbury Town. As we'd already played them twice (and beaten them twice too!) we didn't need to worry about his team stitching us up, but as Shrewsbury still had to play both Stockport and Rushden and Diamonds we hoped they'd do us a favour and take three points off them. To find out if they did, all you have to do is read on.

> **March Quotes:**
>
> *"If I have to pay the money myself, I'll appeal!"*
> **Corny was sure Lee Thorpe's sending off against Chester could be overturned. After seeing the match video he realised there was no point appealing.**
>
> *"These last few games aren't going to be pretty!"*
> **Corny's prediction after the win at Wycombe. Unfortunately he was destined to watch them on TV after Ian Atkins was asked to take over.**

March Stats

matches	won	drew	lost	league points	league placing
3	2	0	1	7	up 1

goals scored	scorers:	goals conceded
3	Bedeau (2) Hill	1

players used	19
average match time in possession of ball	47%

yellow cards	red cards
2	1

fouls	by United	by opponents
	32	36

goal attempts	by United	by opponents
	22	32

total attendance	total miles travelled
11,378	920
Ave: 3,793	

Table at end of March

	P	W	D	L	F	A	GD	Pts
Carlisle Utd	39	22	8	9	76	37	39	74
Grimsby Town	39	20	8	11	58	40	18	68
Northampton	39	17	15	7	52	33	19	66
Leyton Orient	39	18	12	9	57	46	11	66
Wycombe W.	39	16	17	6	65	45	20	65
Cheltenham	39	16	13	10	52	45	7	61
Peterborough	39	15	11	13	50	39	11	56
Lincoln City	39	13	17	9	55	45	10	56
Wrexham	38	14	12	12	55	43	12	54
Bristol Rovers	39	15	8	16	50	57	-7	53
Darlington	39	12	13	13	45	43	2	49
Mansfield T.	39	12	12	15	56	57	-1	48
Shrewsbury	39	12	12	15	44	48	-4	48
Boston United	39	11	15	13	43	54	-11	48
Notts County	39	12	12	15	41	52	-11	48
Rochdale	37	12	9	16	57	59	-2	45
Macclesfield	38	10	15	13	50	59	-9	45
Oxford United	39	10	15	14	37	47	-10	45
Stockport C.	38	9	16	13	49	66	-17	43
Bury	38	10	12	16	37	49	-12	42
Barnet	38	9	15	14	37	50	-13	42
Chester City	38	10	10	18	47	55	-8	40
Torquay Utd	**38**	**9**	**12**	**17**	**42**	**60**	**-18**	**39**
Rushden/D.	39	9	11	19	38	64	-26	38

March

Nickname Quiz

Can you draw lines to join the nickname to the Div 2 club???

Mansfield Town	*Pilgrims*
Walsall	*Bees*
Macclesfield Town	*Quakers*
Notts County	*Stags*
Boston United	*Saddlers*
Bury	*Exiles*
Barnet	*Silkmen*
Chester City	*Magpies*
Darlington	*Shakers*

what???

Grounds Quiz

Now do the same with these grounds. Oh stop moaning for goodness sake! Honestly, you do go on you know!

Memorial Stadium	**Shrewsbury Town**
Edgeley Park	**Rochdale**
Nene Park	**Wrexham**
Gay Meadow	**Stockport County**
Racecourse Ground	**Rushden and Diamonds**
Spotland	**Bristol Rovers**

The Ref!

Love him or hate him (and it's usually the latter), no game can take place without our friend in black (or green, or yellow ..... we'll come to that one later). He can be your best mate / saviour / hero one minute, and your worst enemy the next. One thing's for certain - in any match on any Saturday afternoon he'll take more stick than all the players, coaches and chairmen put together.

SO WHY DOES HE DO IT???

To find out more about this strange, masochistic humanoid life form we met up with Football League Referee Iain Williamson before the home game against Grimsby in January.

Fact File:

Name: Iain Williamson   **Age:** 35

Full-time Job: Head of Key Accounts at Birmingham Midshires Solutions

Background: Played for Walton and Hersham in Isthmian League. Started refereeing after knee injury cut short playing career.

Current Status: Band 'A' referee. These are the top 12 refs below the fully-contracted panel.

Q. *Iain. How did you get to be a league ref?*

Well, like all other refs I started out in charge of local league games on park pitches. After assessments at each level I moved up from Class 3, through Classes 2 and 1 and onto the Suburban League, refereeing Isthmian League reserve fixtures. After seven years I'd worked my way up to Conference League level, before refereeing my first Football League game in 2002. As a member of the National List I can be asked to take charge of Coca Cola, Carling Cup, FA Cup or even Premiership matches, or to be an Assistant Referee or Fourth Official at any of these levels. (Full National List refs can be allocated to matches all over the country, whereas Assistant Refs are only given games up to 120 miles from their home).

Q. *What's the next step for you?*

I'm currently a member of the Development Group of 12 refs who are being prepared for Premiership level games. If I reach that level I hope to be nominated to the FIFA list. The cut-off age for that is 40, which gives me 5 years to reach my target. Retirement ages are 45 for FIFA matches and 48 for FA Premier League matches.

Q. *How fit do you need to be to be a ref?*

Pretty fit! Every summer all the football league refs meet up to take the Cooper Test. To pass this you need to run 2700 metres in 12 minutes. Basically that means keeping going at a steady tough pace from start to finish.

Q. *What if you fail?*

It's two strikes and you're out! Fail the first time and you're given a special training programme to prepare you for the retest. In the meantime you're not allowed to referee any games. Fail the second time and you have to wait till next season.

Q. *What training do you need to do to keep match fit during the season?*

I train two or three times a week, wired up to a heart-rate monitor and trying to copy the intensity that I would experience in an actual game. That's really important because during a match I wear a special watch and monitor which record my movements and heart-rate. This data is then sent to a fitness advisor for analysis to make sure that:

a)   I'm working hard enough to keep up with play effectively.

b)   My work rate is consistent during the whole 90 minutes, and I'm not taking it easy for part of the game to make sure I've still got enough energy for the closing stages.

You can't hide from the truth, and the data never lies!

Q. *What preparation do you do before a match?*

I generally find out which matches I'm going to be reffing one month in advance (Premiership is only one week in advance). I only start preparing myself for a match once the previous game is out of the way, so that it gets my all of my attention. Then I try to gather information which will give me a clue as to how each team plays and what kind of game I can expect. I'll look up match reports, visit club and FA websites and speak to refs who've done the teams' recent matches.

For instance, my notes for the Grimsby game included:

● Grimsby have the best defensive record in the division, with only one away defeat at Wycombe, so are likely to be well-organised and difficult to break down.

● They're a massive team with nearly every player over six foot, so may well play the ball in the air a lot. Torquay are relatively small and have a reputation for wanting to keep the ball on the deck. A classic clash of playing styles.

- Grimsby's leading score, Reddy, has been offside 38 times already this season, so seems to be a gambler on the edge of the offside trap. I'll need to tell my assistants about that.

- Both teams have fairly average disciplinary records (Grimsby 38 Yellows and 3 Reds, Torquay 41 and 3), so neither appears to be what you might call a 'dirty' side.

- Grimsby have two players on 4 yellow cards, which may affect their performance as 5 yellows means an automatic suspension. For Torquay Matt Hewlett has already served a ban for 5 yellows, so he might be a player who likes to get stuck in. (the data doesn't always show whether previous yellows are for foul play or dissent).

This information starts to build up a picture in my mind that Grimsby may well like to take a more direct route to goal with more through balls and crosses fired in, whereas Torquay may prefer a more patient approach, passing the ball around and waiting for an opening. If that's the case, much will depend on the weather and the condition of the pitch - wind, rain and a cut-up pitch will probably favour Grimsby.

Q. *What's your routine on match day?*

12:30 Arrive at the ground. I'll introduce myself to the club Secretary or General Manager (ie Debbie Hancox) then have a quick look round the pitch and changing rooms. The kit will probably have been laid out by then so I'll be able to see if there are any clashes. At the Grimsby match both goalies had silver shirts laid out, so the away goalie had to be asked to change. It's the responsibility of the away team to contact the home team in the week before the game to make sure this doesn't happen. (Oops!)

I can then also decide what colour shirt to wear myself. In this case, as Torquay play in yellow and Grimsby in black and white, I'll wear green. Personally I think refs should always wear the traditional black.

Unfortunately this had to change when Manchester United got the permission of the FA to have a black kit. [Another triumph of money and commercialism over tradition! AB] After this I'll meet my team of officials as well as the Match Assessor, who is also part of the team, (my performance in every game is assessed on a points system by an ex ref) and we'll have a cup of tea and discuss the game.

1:45 Following a more thorough pitch inspection we'll meet the police or security team. They'll run through various details with us, such as:

- how many away fans are expected
- what the emergency evacuation procedures are in the case of fire or bomb scare
- what will happen if I or my officials need to be escorted from the pitch at half- or full-time.
- where the First Aiders will be situated

2:00 Meet the two coaches and captains, receive the team sheets and answer any questions.

2:54 Call the teams from the changing rooms and get out on the pitch.

3:45 During half-time I'll take in plenty of fluids to guard against dehydration and discuss with my team how the first half went, whether any players stand out for closer attention and what we might expect in the rest of the match. The second half is nearly always more difficult to ref than the first, as the tension and intensity rise towards the end of the game and some tempers tend to get a little frayed. Neither players nor coaches are allowed into my office to speak to me at half-time.

4:50 Game over. No coach is allowed to speak to me for 30 minutes following the final whistle (in actual fact very few of them choose to speak to me after that). We do not accept video evidence from coaches' laptops after the game, and cannot now agree to check videos to reassess red or yellow cards - that's the responsibility of a separate FA panel.

5:15 My assessor will come in to discuss my performance with me.

Q. *How do you decide how much time needs to be added on at the end of each half?*

I keep a mental note of any time wasting or delays that need added time, and every substitution puts another 30 seconds on. Each time a trainer comes on for an injury I'll add on time depending on how long it takes to treat the player on the pitch. A few minutes from the end of each half I'll signal the number of added minutes to the fourth official either by buzzing him or with a hand gesture.

Q. *How do you deal with dissent from players?*

Generally by using common sense. Players are not angels, and they're in a highly emotional state during a game. It's understandable that they may not always choose their words over-carefully. Having said that, you have to draw the line between bad language on the spur of the moment and downright foul abuse, which merits a yellow or even red card.

Q. *Do you hear the fans' comments during a match?*

Not really, no. The voices do get through but they're blurred, especially if there's a big crowd - I'm concentrating too hard on the game. In a small ground, or during stoppages in play, then yes I do hear what people have to say. It's all part of the job. Sometimes the comments genuinely make me laugh or smile - there are some very amusing people in those stands!

Q. *How do you manage to keep up with play during a game?*

The tactic is always to try to keep the play between yourself and an assistant, so that we've both got a view of the action, one from each side (each assistant has an electronic buzzer in their flag which transmits to a vibrating pad on my arm, so they can communicate with me instantly). To do this effectively I try as much as possible to move along a diagonal or S shape as shown in the diagram below:

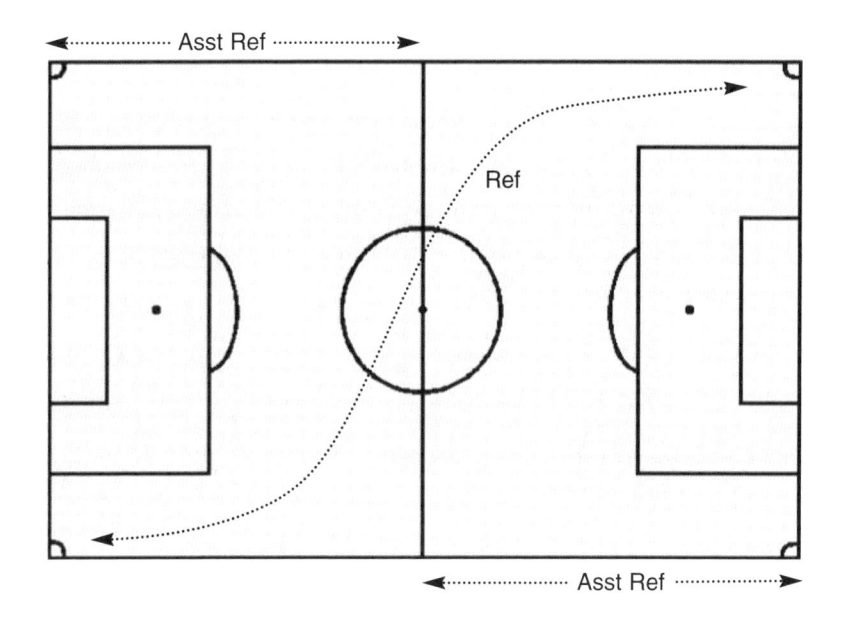

Q. How do you know when to give a red or yellow card for a foul?

Fouls generally fall into three categories:

Carelessness	A clumsy challenge with no real intent to foul. Give a free kick and talk to the player.
Recklessness	More of a wild challenge that is dangerous, with some intent to foul, including tackles from behind. Yellow card.
Disproportionate Force	Player goes into challenge with clear intent to hurt opponent, possibly seriously. Red card.

Q. What about bookings for goal celebrations?

Firstly, let me assure you that contrary to what some fans might think, we are not spoilsports who don't like to see players have fun! Football is a highly charged game, and we understand the emotions going through the mind of a player who's just scored, especially if it's a vital goal. They're on a high, and that's great. The laws on goal celebrations revolve mostly around crowd safety issues:

A player running up to the edge of his own crowd and beckoning to them causes fans to run or push down towards the front of the terracing. This can easily result in injuries from crushing. Even more dangerous is a player running or jumping *into* his own fans. Both of these celebrations mean a yellow card for the scorer.

A scorer who taunts the *opposition* fans or makes an abusive gesture to them must be given the red card .... if the ref sees it.

A player pulling his shirt over his head receives no punishment, but a scorer taking his shirt off [who could ever forget Giggsy's chest rug?? AB] gets a yellow.

Q. *What's the 4th Official's job during a game?*

He (or she) has various duties:

● to manage substitutes. Each team has three blue cards, on which they write the numbers of the player to come off and the one to go on. They *must* give one of these cards to the 4th Official before they can make a substitution (teams have been known to lose these cards and so not be able to make any subs!). The 4th Official will then hold up the electronic board with the players' numbers on it to show who's coming off and who's going on.

● to signal how many minutes of added time there will be at the end of each half.

● to keep an eye on the coaches, make sure they stay in their technical areas, monitor their comments to ref and assistants and try to keep thcm as calm as possible! (Some offer coaches a sweet or have a laugh with them to defuse situations. Some don't.)

- to make sure that no more than two officials from each bench are standing up at any one time.

- to keep an eye on events in the tunnel at half-time and full-time. If there is any trouble they are there as observers only - for safety reasons they must not intervene. Any incidents are passed on to the ref and will go into his match report.

- to step in if there is an injury to either the ref or one of his assistants. If the ref can't carry on the Senior Assistant (who always runs the line on the dug-out side of the pitch) will take over as ref, and the 4th Official will run the line.

Q. *What happens after you leave?*

I need to write my match report, which will include information about the weather, pitch and facilities at the ground. I need to inform the FA by the following day of any yellow or red cards I've given out.

Each club will have their own report to fill in about my performance. Obviously it's important that they're honest. Nobody's perfect, all refs make mistakes and all good refs try to learn from them. As far as I'm concerned I go away from a ground happy if everyone feels they've been treated fairly, and that whether they won or lost it was down to their own performance and not mine. If players or fans are talking about me rather than the football, then something's gone wrong. My aim is to turn up, referee the game and go home again without anyone knowing I've been there!

....

Thanks Iain. It's great to hear all this information first hand. I'm sure we'll all be much more tolerant and polite towards referees from now on. (Yeh, right!!!)

Now You're The Ref!

Most of us take great delight in slagging off the poor old ref - he must be blind, daft, biased, etc. But how would you cope if you were the one with the whistle and an angry crowd screaming at you? What decision would you give in these situations:

1. United are awarded an indirect free kick just outside the box following an obstruction. Darren Garner crosses, aiming for the head of Lee Thorpe, but the ball misses everyone, just brushing the shirt of a defender on its way into the goal. **Your decision?**

2. Kevin Hill has been injured in a goalmouth challenge. He goes off the pitch behind the goal to get treatment from physio Darren James. Seeing United coming forward again he runs back onto the pitch into an onside position, just in time to meet Buster's cross and send a header bulleting into the top corner of the net. **Decision?**

3. Steven Reed takes a long throw which bounces over everyone's head, including the goaly's, and bobbles into the empty net. We know it's no goal, but how should the game restart? **Well??**

4. Torquay's goaly hoofs a goal-kick upfield. Mickey Evans is the only player from either side in the opposition half (except their goaly). The ball clears everybody and lands at Micky's feet, just outside the opposition penalty area. He pulls the ball down and hammers it past the keeper into the roof of the net. **Whaddaya say, smarty pants???**

(see page 158 for answers)

April

FOURTH STRAIGHT DEFEAT SENDS GULLS DOWN!

Going ..... Going ..... Gone!!!

CONFERENCE HERE WE COME!

Be honest, how many of you expected to see headlines like this halfway through April? If you didn't, I take my hat off to you – you're exactly the type of fan that all clubs need, someone who NEVER admits defeat and ALWAYS believes that things will work out. For you the glass is always half full instead of half empty (Tip: if it still looks half full after you've drunk it all then you're either a super optimist or you need to see an optician [question: if you *really* need to see an optician, how can you be absolutely sure that the person you see is actually the optician??? AB]) (Is that enough brackets or do you think I should put a few more in?) ([]()

With the postponement of the Stockport game at the end of March United had an unwanted two-week break before the crucial Rushden game. It would have been great to build on the confidence gained from the Wycombe win by thrashing Stockport at home and marching into April on the back of three consecutive wins. The delay blunted our cutting edge as well as allowing other teams to pick up points on us, and made the trip to Rushden even more of a six-pointer than it was already.

For a long away journey like this one, the team would normally travel up on the Friday, do a spot of training, relax at a hotel and then play the game on the Saturday. Up to this point Torquay's record of such Friday away trips was Played 7, Drawn 2, Lost 5. The players got their heads together and came up with the suggestion that it might be better to change the routine and travel up Saturday morning instead. It would mean an early start and a long coach ride on the morning before the match, but it was certainly worth a try to break the unlucky sequence. In the event it didn't work. Typically for this time of year the strong wind made good football difficult, but United had the chances to get all three points. The Diamonds lost their goaly after half an hour, and Torquay had 61% of possession to Rushden's 39%. As so often though they failed to turn possession into goals, and the saddest statistic was that with all the ball they had, United failed to put a single effort on target in the whole match. I doubt if Rushden's sub goaly could believe his luck – he must've been a bag of nerves when he had to come on in such a vital match, then he didn't have a save to make in the entire game! With Broughton heading in from a corner at the end of the first half United trudged disconsolately off at the end, knowing that the loss sent Rushden back above them and left them back on the bottom. When there are only seven games to go, that's not where you want to be.

With two home games coming up manager John Cornforth would have been hoping for the full six points, and for awhile against Darlington it looked as if he would get at least three of them. United ripped into the visitors right from the off, and could have been three up in the first half hour. The pressure finally told after 37 minutes when Kevin Hill rose like a jet-powered salmon to power a header into the roof of the net from Reed's far-post corner. It was no more than United deserved – they were playing all the football, treating the crowd to a great display of passing and movement, and rightly left the pitch to a standing ovation at half-time. The game should have been all over, done and dusted, but instead the second half saw a return to the bad old days, with United sitting back and allowing the opposition to get on top and swarm forward like angry bees. Suddenly every 50/50 tackle was going Darlington's way, and every loose ball was being gobbled up by a black and white shirt. It was only a matter of time before the equaliser came, and you just knew it wouldn't end there. Sure enough, with two minutes to go Marriott saved superbly from a corner, only for the ball to run to Wainwright, who thumped an unstoppable drive into the top corner for the winner. At the final whistle the fans made their disappointment clear – the team had seemed to go down without a fight in the second half. They couldn't expect to do that and survive the drop.

The price for the defeat was the dismissal of the unfortunate John Cornforth. After a promising start things hadn't quite worked out. Mike Bateson admitted that his experiment with a manager/football advisor partnership hadn't worked, and Ian Atkins was asked to take on the job of coach until the end of the season. Atkins had been in this situation before, and it was thought that his greater experience of leading clubs through a crisis could prove vital with United in such a perilous position.

> *A ventriloquist is doing a show in London.*
> **Chelsea fan**: *Oi! You on stage! You've been making jokes about Chelsea all night! Pack it in, will you!*
> **Ventriloquist**: *Relax mate, it's only a bit of fun!*
> **Chelsea fan**: *I'm not talking to you, I'm talking to that ugly little bloke on your knee!*

Joke!

Have you ever heard of déjà vu? No, it's not Arsenal's latest signing or an Italian pasta dish made with carrots, anchovies and snails, it's that weird feeling you sometimes get that you've seen something or been somewhere before. It used to happen to me in tests. I'd open the paper, start reading and immediately think: 'Uh-oh, I've seen this question before. I couldn't answer it that time either.'

Well, visitors to Plainmoor for the Cheltenham game could be forgiven for thinking that the whole afternoon was one long déjà vu. Connell was given a start up front, and with Thorpe a constant threat United began brightly. As the half wore on they got more and more on top, and in the 26th minute Thorpe coolly raced clear, flicked the ball over the stranded goaly and knocked it into the empty net to send the crowd into raptures of delight. This time Torquay came out for the second half with much more determination, clearly having learned their lesson from the previous week. After 60 minutes, however, it was a case of 'Oh no, here we go again!' as Spencer headed an equaliser for Cheltenham. United poured forward in search of a winner but ten minutes later were hit by a sucker punch when Odejayi beat the offside trap and lobbed over Marriott from thirty yards. Despite continuous pressure and three late substitutions the ball wouldn't go in the net, and once again the Gulls had snatched defeat from the jaws of victory.

Isn't it strange how matches at the end of the season seem to take on so much more meaning than those earlier on? At the end of the game people were muttering darkly that the loss of those three points would be the reason why Torquay would be playing Conference football next season. How many people mentioned the three points dropped when United blew a two-goal lead in the last fifteen minutes against Bristol Rovers back in August? After all, three points is three points, whether it's from the first game of the season or the last. Isn't it?

With Stockport and Oxford both winning and Rushden only being denied a victory by a last-gasp Rochdale equaliser, Torquay's defeat left the bottom of the table looking like this:

	P	W	D	L	F	A	GD	Pts
Macclesfield	42	11	17	14	54	63	-9	50
Notts County	42	12	14	16	44	56	-12	50
Oxford United	42	11	15	16	39	49	-10	48
Bury	42	11	14	17	40	53	-13	47
Stockport C.	41	10	17	14	54	71	-17	47
Barnet	41	10	15	16	40	55	-15	45
Rushden/D.	42	11	12	19	41	65	-24	45
Torquay Utd	**41**	**9**	**12**	**20**	**44**	**65**	**-21**	**39**

Was this the darkest hour? Five games to go, six points adrift at the foot of the league, three defeats on the trot and on their third manager of the season, you could be forgiven for believing that United were doomed. Certainly that seemed to be the opinion around the country. If you cared to listen to supporters of other clubs it was now only a question of who would go down with us.

Maybe that helped in a funny kind of way. Nobody expected us to survive, so we had nothing to lose. One thing seemed certain. If United lost at Macclesfield in their next match it really would be all over. The fat lady had already finished her warm-up, put the music on the stand in front of her and taken a deep breath, just waiting for the signal from the conductor. The time had surely come ......

Manager Atkins restored proven goalscorer Tony Bedeau to the attack to play alongside Lee Thorpe. The injury which led to his departure after only half an hour seemed to be the final nail in the coffin, but it turned out to be exactly the opposite when replacement Jo Kuffour stabbed the ball home from a Thorpe knock down early in the second half. Then it was all hands to the pump as Macclesfield threw everything at an increasingly desperate United defence. In the hour of need they stood firm, and the evening was capped when Kuffour sprinted clear at the death to calmly stroke the ball past Lee and into the bottom corner. We were still alive!!!

Other results were mixed, with Notts County and Barnet both winning but Stockport and Oxford losing. When Rushden were hammered 4-1 by Leroy's Shrewsbury the following night the table had reformed to:

	P	W	D	L	F	A	GD	Pts
Macclesfield	43	11	17	15	54	65	-11	50
Notts County	43	12	14	17	45	58	-13	50
Oxford United	43	11	15	17	39	50	-11	48
Bury	43	11	15	17	40	53	-13	48
Barnet	42	11	15	16	41	55	-14	48
Stockport C.	42	10	17	15	54	73	-19	47
Rushden/D.	43	11	12	20	42	69	-27	45
Torquay Utd	**42**	**10**	**12**	**20**	**46**	**65**	**-19**	**42**

Still grim reading, but not quite as grim as it had been two days earlier. In our favour was the fact that three of our last four games were at home. If only we could just put a run together. Wrexham were the visitors on the Saturday. Although down in tenth place in the table they still held hopes of a play-off place, so they had plenty to play for. The Gulls began positively and Woods' quick thinking nearly got them off to a dream start when his Beckham-ish snapshot from all of 55 yards shaved the Wrexham bar. The all important first goal came shortly afterwards though, when Buster Phillips seized on a loose ball and drove it past goalkeeper Jones from close range after only nine minutes. Round about this point the nerves appeared to set in, because after that there was a lot of heavy traffic bearing down on the Torquay goal and only a few bikes and a Mini Cooper heading in the opposite direction. Taylor and Woods were superb in the centre of defence (how many times would we say that before the end of the season??) and the equaliser that would have broken our hearts never arrived.

The sigh of relief at the final whistle could be heard as far away as

Rushden and Diamonds, whose defeat at home to Wycombe dumped them down below us again on goal difference. Oxford and Macclesfield both lost, there were draws for Notts County and Barnet and Stockport won:

	P	W	D	L	F	A	GD	Pts
Bury	44	12	14	17	43	55	-12	51
Notts County	44	12	15	17	46	59	-13	51
Macclesfield	44	11	17	16	56	68	-12	50
Stockport C.	43	11	17	15	57	74	-17	50
Barnet	43	11	16	16	41	55	-14	49
Oxford United	44	11	15	18	40	53	-13	48
Torquay Utd	**43**	**11**	**12**	**20**	**47**	**65**	**-18**	**45**
Rushden/D.	44	11	12	21	43	72	-29	45

That was how things looked as we prepared ourselves for the night of the season, the Tuesday evening showdown, the crunch game at home to Stockport County. The record until then in evening games didn't look promising: Played 9, Drawn 5, Lost 4, Won ......0.

In games like these the team that scores first often goes on to win. We'd found from recent home games that wasn't always the case with United, so to be on the safe side they they got the first, second and third goals, all in the first 23 minutes! Stockport just didn't know what hit 'em as they were blitzed right from the kick off. Whatever it was that Ian Atkins put in their pre-match cup of tea, he should bottle it and sell it down at Boots – he'd make a fortune! On the biggest stage of the season Lee Thorpe played the lead role, setting the scene with a spectacular overhead kick to open the scoring after just four minutes, and then rifling a header past the helpless Spencer from a Darren Garner corner. It was Jo Kuffour's turn to get in on the act next, as he again used his pace to beat the offside trap before crashing the ball into the roof of the net for number three. In the stand grown men were crying with joy as the Gulls turned on the style with a vintage display of champagne football.

Stockport no doubt got a roasting from their boss at half-time, and came out determined to put matters right in the second half. Instead it was United that shut the door firmly in their face when Danny Hollands grabbed his first goal for the club, guiding a classy volley over the head of Spencer in goal. It was probably asking too much for the scoring to carry on to the end of the match, but Atkins would have impressed on his team the need to keep a clean sheet. With so many clubs sandwiched together at the bottom, relegation might come down to goal difference, and so Andy Marriott's brilliant tip-over from Dickinson's last-minute header was just as important as any of United's goals.

The 3565 fans (the biggest home league gate of the season) had witnessed one of the great United performances, especially given the pressure the team were under, and Tuesday 25th April 2006 will be a night talked about for many years to come.

One thing the victory didn't do was move United any further up the table. They moved level on points with Oxford, one goal behind them on goal difference, but still two points adrift of Stockport, Macclesfield and Barnet, who picked up a vital point at Rochdale:

	P	W	D	L	F	A	GD	Pts
Bury	44	12	15	17	43	55	-12	51
Notts County	44	12	15	17	46	59	-13	51
Macclesfield	44	11	17	16	56	68	-12	50
Barnet	44	11	17	16	42	56	-14	50
Stockport C.	44	11	17	16	57	78	-21	50
Oxford United	44	11	15	18	40	53	-13	48
Torquay Utd	**44**	**12**	**12**	**20**	**51**	**65**	**-14**	**48**
Rushden/D.	44	11	12	21	43	72	-29	45

So we were still in one of the two relegation spots. With a visit to top of the table Carlisle to come at the weekend, we were far from out of the woods yet. We desperately needed at least a point from that game to make sure that all the heroics of the Stockport game didn't go to waste.

Breaking their previous away trip routine United made the long journey up to Carlisle on the Thursday evening, arriving late at night. That gave them a full day to train, get the coach journey out of their system and then relax before the big game. Bedeau had not recovered and so Kuffour kept his place in the starting line-up. Lee Andrews, on loan from Carlisle, wasn't allowed to play against his own club (one of the drawbacks of loan deals) and so Matt Villis again stepped into the defensive unit.

A noisy crowd of well over 13,000 turned up, clearly expecting to witness the victory which would see Carlisle crowned as Division 2 champions. Maybe someone forgot to tell the Torquay players that the afternoon was supposed to be one big party, however, because they carried on where they'd left off against Stockport. Kuffour crossed for Hill to once again show off his skill in the air and head home. One up after eight minutes! Kuffour rattled the woodwork as United surged forward, then swivelled and cracked a low drive in off the post to send United two up just before half-time. This was all too much for the home crowd, who showed their team what they thought with a chorus of boos as they left the pitch. The plan for the second half was clear. Soak up everything Carlisle could throw at them without conceding a goal, then try to push forward again and hit them on the break. Sometimes even the best plans don't quite work. The home team pulled one back within three minutes of the restart, and we feared the worst. Spurred on by their baying fans Carlisle tore into Torquay, but once again Taylor and Woods led the defence brilliantly and refused to buckle under the intense pressure. When the final whistle eventually came it must've sounded like the ding of the bell to a battered boxer on the ropes. They'd done it! Against all odds they'd notched up their fourth straight win and beaten the top team on their own patch. Even the Carlisle fans showed their respect by giving the United players and supporters a great hand – they knew from experience what it was like both to survive and to go down on the last day of the season.

After the smoke had cleared we could start to relax and look at the other results coming in. Barnet, Stockport, Macclesfield and Oxford had all drawn, Notts County had lost and Rushden were relegated following their defeat at Boston. We rubbed our eyes and studied this new-look table in disbelief....

	P	W	D	L	F	A	GD	Pts
Bury	45	12	16	17	43	55	-12	52
Macclesfield	45	11	18	16	57	69	-12	51
Torquay Utd	**45**	**13**	**12**	**20**	**53**	**66**	**-13**	**51**
Barnet	45	11	18	16	42	56	-14	51
Notts County	45	12	15	18	46	61	-15	51
Stockport C.	45	11	18	16	57	78	-21	51
Oxford United	45	11	16	18	41	54	-13	49
Rushden/D.	45	11	12	22	43	74	-31	45

United had jumped up to nineteenth in the league! What a time to achieve your highest position all season – right when it mattered most. Surely we were safe now? The fat lady was already picking her music up and starting to shuffle off the stage, muttering something about 'lucky Gulls!' It's not luck, missus, it's skill and fighting spirit!

April Quotes:

"The pressure on Notts County, Macclesfield, Barnet and Oxford is tremendous - while the cooker's off us, they're in the heat now !"

Ian Atkins plays mind games with the other relegation candidates following the memorable 4-0 win over Stockport County.

April Stats

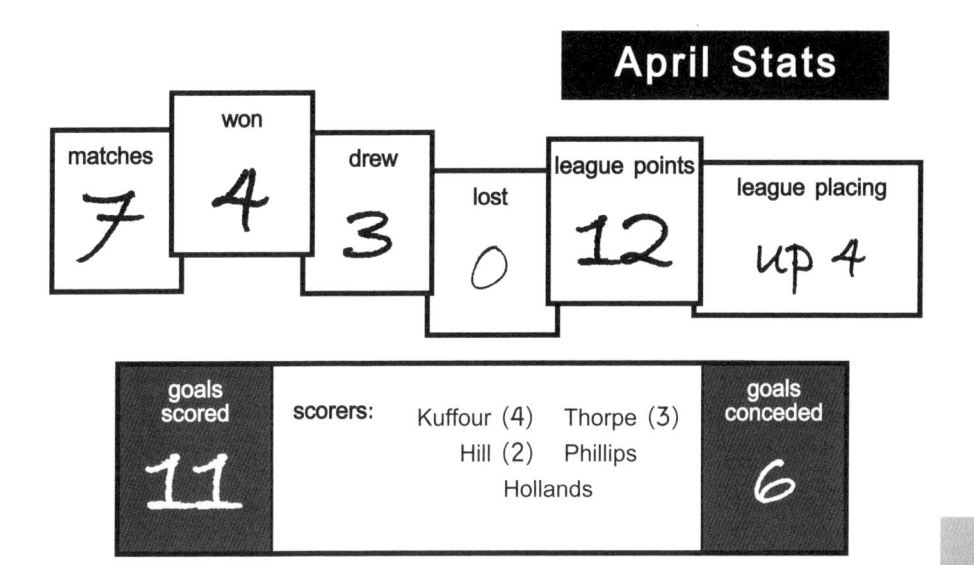

matches	won	drew	lost	league points	league placing
7	4	3	0	12	up 4

goals scored: 11

scorers: Kuffour (4)   Thorpe (3)   Hill (2)   Phillips   Hollands

goals conceded: 6

players used	19
average match time in possession of ball	53%

yellow cards	red cards
4	0

fouls	by United	by opponents
	75	81

goal attempts	by United	by opponents
	57	77

total attendance	total miles travelled
31,309	1,709
Ave: 4,473	

Table at end of April

	P	W	D	L	F	A	GD	Pts
Carlisle Utd	44	24	10	10	82	42	40	82
Northampton	45	22	16	7	62	36	26	82
Leyton Orient	45	21	15	9	64	49	15	78
Grimsby Town	45	22	11	12	63	43	20	77
Cheltenham	45	18	15	12	60	53	7	69
Wycombe W.	45	17	17	11	70	56	20	68
Lincoln City	45	15	20	10	64	52	12	65
Peterborough	45	17	11	17	57	47	10	62
Darlington	45	16	14	15	57	51	6	62
Bristol Rovers	45	17	9	19	57	64	-7	60
Boston United	45	15	15	15	50	60	-10	60
Wrexham	45	15	13	17	60	53	7	58
Shrewsbury	45	15	13	17	54	55	-1	58
Rochdale	44	14	13	17	65	66	-1	55
Mansfield Town	45	13	15	17	59	61	-2	54
Chester City	45	14	12	19	53	58	-5	54
Bury	45	12	16	17	43	55	-12	52
Macclesfield	45	11	18	16	57	69	-12	51
Torquay Utd	**45**	**13**	**12**	**20**	**53**	**66**	**-13**	**51**
Barnet	45	11	18	16	42	56	-14	51
Notts County	45	12	15	18	46	61	-15	51
Stockport C.	45	11	18	16	57	78	-21	51
Oxford United	45	11	16	18	41	54	-13	49
Rushden/D.	45	11	12	22	43	74	-31	45

April

CAN YOU WORK OUT THE AREA OF THIS CENTRE CIRCLE?

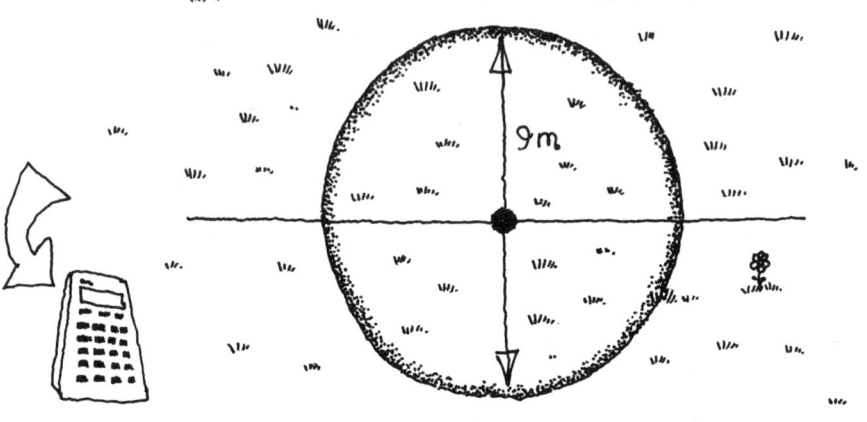

9m

AB'S TIP!

To CALCULATE THE AREA OF A CIRCLE YOU USE $pi \ r^2$
(In other words, square the radius of the circle, then multiply that by pi, which is 3.14)
By the way, the radius is half the diameter!

So .....

The area of the circle is...

TOTAL

CAN YOU BELIEVE THAT?? (2)
(find out on page 158...)

> **fact**
> PI IS WHAT'S KNOWN AS A CONSTANT...
> It doesn't change. It's usually rounded down to 2 decimal places, 3.14, though a computer has calculated it to 1,241,100,000,000 decimal places!

The world record for memorising the value of Pi is held by a Japanese man called AKIRA HARAGUCHI, who on 1st July 2005 recited the first 83,431 decimal places from memory..... while standing on his head in a bath of baked beans! ← **mad fact!**

NOW USING Pi AGAIN.....
Can you calculate the circumference of the circle?
(that's the distance around the edge!)
ANSWER: Yes, you can! This time you use the formula:

→ **2 pi r or pi d (pi x diameter)**

Come on then, clever clogs, lets see you do this one without a calculator!....

TOTAL

Look at this diagram of a football pitch. Can you work out how far you'd run if you sprinted from one corner to the corner diagonally opposite?

65 m

105 m

?

ancient Greek dude!

*
ΘΥ!॥⚹
mх⚹6
♎!!·Ⅲ
m# ⊕#॥
6⚹!!...

AB's TIP!

To calculate this you need to listen to that Ancient Greek dude PYTHAGORAS, who showed that in a right angle triangle, the square of the length of the hypotenuse (the long side) is equal to the squares of the other two sides added together. If that's a bit confusing, look at this:

3 squared = 9   4 squared = 16

9 + 16 = 25, which is 5 squared!

3

?

4

So after that, the length of the diagonal is......

Rounded to 3 decimal places. ☐

Rounded to 1 decimal place. ☐

* over 'ere son, on me 'ead!!

International clairvoyant to the stars!

Looking back into my crystal ball, I see great success for United in their third Premiership season of 2014. Having reached the semi-finals of the Champions League, only to be knocked out by a late dodgy penalty for Real Madrid the Gulls finished the season with 8 straight league wins to clinch a magnificent first Premiership title. The table below shows just how dominant they were, though some interfering kid has rubbed out some of the figures.

Can you fill in the empty boxes? (You'll need the clues underneath!)

	P	W	D	L	F	A	GD	Pts
Torquay Utd	38	28	7	3	97		52	
Man Utd	38			9	73	43	30	73
West Ham Utd	38	21			58	43	15	69
Spurs	38	19	10	9	51	30	21	
Aston Villa	38	18	11	9	53			65
Liverpool	38		13		46	35	11	58
Watford	38	16	10	12	57	56	1	
Middlesborough	38			15	55	55	0	55
Macclesfield	38	15	10	13	52	53	-1	55
Bolton Wanderers	38	15	8	15			8	53
Blackburn Rovers	38			14	63	54	9	52
Leeds Utd	38	14	10	14		52		52

Clues. (In no particular order!):   *It's that 'Madame Bradbury' she's off again!*

- Man United drew the same number of games as Middlesborough.
- Liverpool won 1 more game than Blackburn.
- West Ham's goal difference was 21 better than Leeds United's.
- Torquay scored 48 more goals than Bolton conceded.
- Middlesborough won 12 fewer games than Torquay.
- Blackburn drew the same number of games as Watford.
- Aston Villa conceded 19 fewer goals than Macclesfield.

133

Imagine you were given the task of team selection for United's last-day match against Boston.

How many different back fours could you make from these six players? (they can all play in any position):

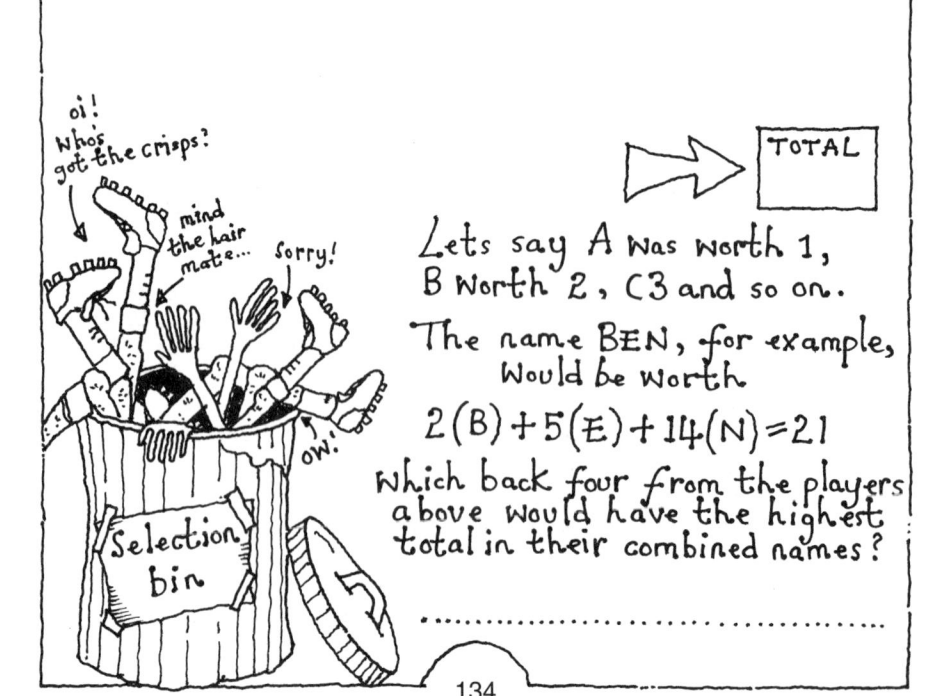

ANDREWS HOCKLEY TAYLOR REED WOODS VILLIS

→ TOTAL

oi! Who's got the crisps?
mind the hair mate...
sorry!
ow!
Selection bin

Lets say A was worth 1, B worth 2, C 3 and so on.

The name BEN, for example, would be worth

$2(B) + 5(E) + 14(N) = 21$

Which back four from the players above would have the highest total in their combined names?

....

These match reports are all taken from last season, but I'm afraid all the words have got muddled up. Can you unscramble them to make proper sentences?

BEWARE! The further you get the trickier they get!

RUBBISH! Please re-type a.s.a.p

The out Marriott air the plucked of easily cross.

....

With area caused throws into Sharp problems long his the.

....

Clinch points three vital out United held to.

....

They the second half Gulls first finished started had the the as.

....

Jo Kuffour's minute got off thanks the flying Gulls start to to a second belter.

....

....

No chance bottom gave corner angled the shot Phillips goalie with an into the.

....

....

135

WARNING!

brains

THIS IS THE TOUGHEST OF THE TOUGH.....

If you can do this one you shouldn't be reading this book. You should be teaching maths in some posh school....

Looking ahead to 2010, there's a bar chart opposite that needs completing, showing the number of games played for the club by various players. You up to it?
ALL YOU NEED TO DO IS READ ALL THE CLUES!! (Maybe in a different order!) THEN DRAW THE BARS (use a ruler!) AND WRITE THE NUMBER OF APPEARANCES IN EACH BAR. AS IN THE EXAMPLE FOR TAYLOR.
(Note the clubs ambitious new signings since being bought out by a consortium containing Russian billionaire Nikolai Avgotanich, and multi-millionaire local businessman Bert Sliggit, owner of Sliggit's Land development and Pasties Ltd

---

- Woodsy has played 84 games more than Matt Hewlett.
- Rooney and Hockley's combined total is 331 games.
- Henry × 5 = Hill + 17.
- Hewlett has played 25 more games than there are days in a leap year.
- (Villis ÷ 2) − 2 = Henry.
- If you divide Woodsy's appearances by 5 and then subtract 8, that's how many games Rooney's played.
- Villis has played 84 games fewer than Hockley.

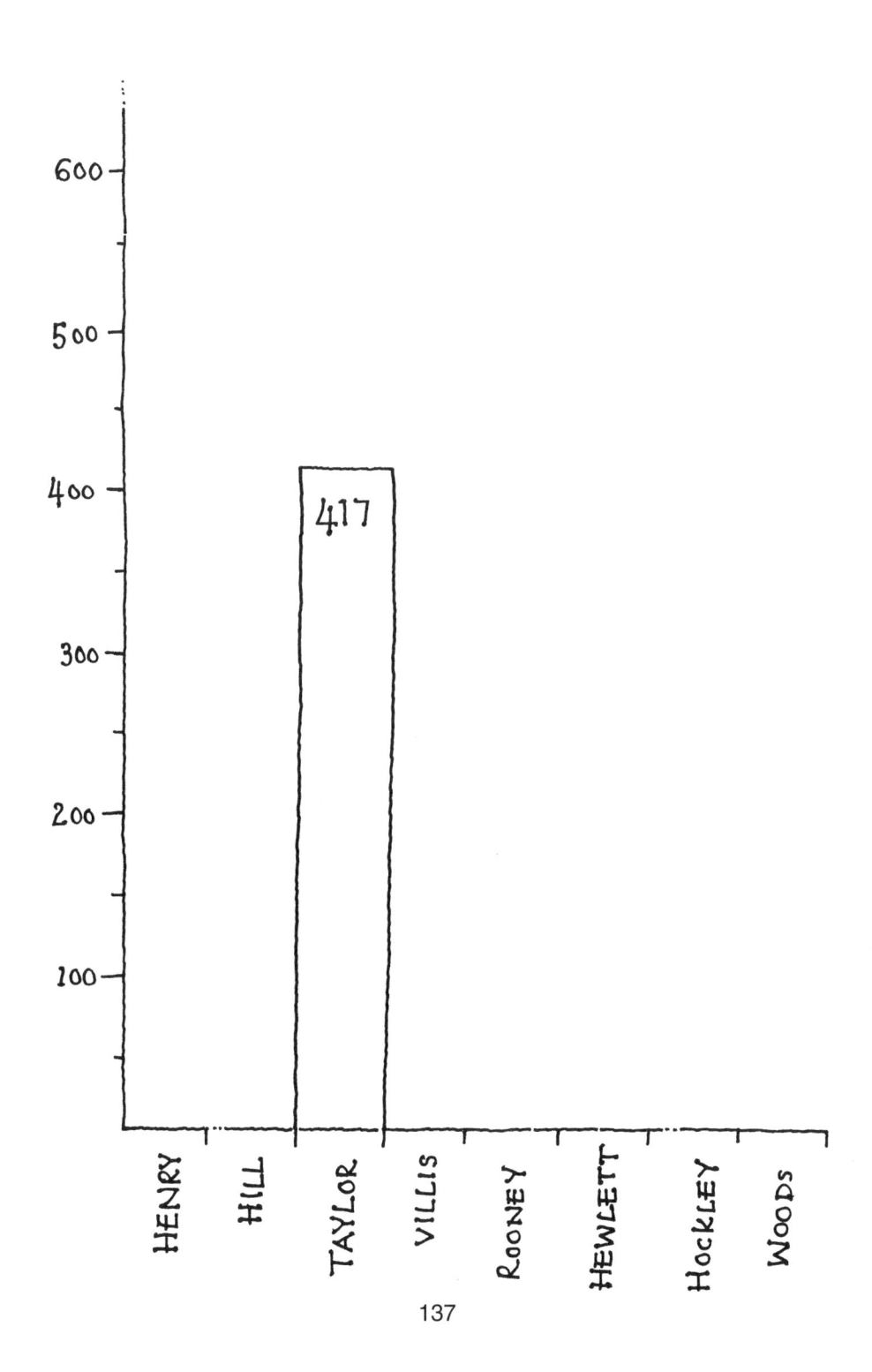

HENRY	HILL	TAYLOR 417	VILLIS	ROONEY	HEWLETT	HOCKLEY	WOODS

May

And so, my friends, it all came down to the last day. Just like in 1957, 1962, 1965 etc etc etc Why does it always seem to happen to Torquay? Wouldn't it be nice to watch the last game of the season without having to care too much about the result .....

"Eee... isn't it lovely to enjoy a nice afternoon out in the sunshine!"

The news before the match was generally good. Ian Atkins had deservedly picked up the Manager of the Month award for April for his Harry Houdini act in plotting the team's dramatic last-ditch escape from the relegation places. The club had managed to claim the away end of

Plainmoor for the home fans, which would not only increase the attendance but improve the atmosphere still further, with Gulls fans on all four sides of the pitch. On top of that, Tony Bedeau had come through a training session and would be on the bench against Boston. On the down side, Buster Phillips would be missing from the line-up, which as we knew from experience would cut down our attacking options drastically. His crosses had been the life blood of our striking partnerships all season – with him out of the team that stream of crosses dried up.

The sunshine of previous days had given way to cloud and drizzle as kick-off approached, but the mood in the ground was anything but dark. It might even be described as festive. Given the results and performances of recent weeks, surely United wouldn't fall at the final fence? After all, they only needed a draw, and if other results went our way we could even lose and still stay up:

- Basically, if Oxford lost or drew against Leyton Orient, we were safe.

- If Oxford won and we only drew, then they'd go above us on goal difference.

- However, with Stockport and Barnet playing each other, it was impossible for both of them to win (derr!). If they drew and we drew we'd still be above both of them on goal difference. If one of them won, the other would still be below us on points.

- BUT .... if Oxford won, Stockport and Barnet drew, Notts County got at least a point, and we lost ..... we were doomed.

Got that? Good! Let's crack on then .....

The United team that took the field showed changes from the Carlisle match, with Lee Andrews returning to the back four in place of Matt Villis and Matt Hockley replacing the injured Buster Phillips in midfield. Right from the start it was clear that this was going to be an edgy affair.

Reluctant to push men forward and risk being caught on the break, most of United's attacks were easily snuffed out by the physical Boston back four. Players looked for the safe option when passing, and the general plan seemed to be "If in doubt, bang the ball up their end of the pitch – they can't score from their own half!" Totally understandable in those circumstances, and while the crowd may have started to get frustrated as move after move broke down, it was always a relief to see the ball around their penalty box rather than ours.

At the back of everyone's minds (actually it was probably right at the front) was the knowledge that a draw would be good enough. It must be so difficult to press forward looking for a winner when you know that it's more important not to concede a goal yourself. If United had needed a win to be sure of safety, or if they'd gone a goal down early on, there's no doubt the game would have turned out entirely differently. As it was, as long as it stayed 0-0 that was fine, and there was no need to do anything silly.

Boston, comfortable in mid-table, had nothing to lose and nothing to play for except pride and enjoyment. They were well-organised and dominated much of the first half with their neat, fluent passing and movement. Fortunately the Torquay defence was equal to all their efforts, Taylor and Woods once again an outstanding partnership in the centre.

After 15 minutes news filtered through that Oxford had taken the lead against Orient, which put them above United on goal difference. A buzz went round the crowd as the news travelled like wild fire – that was one score that was going against us. What we didn't need now was for Notts County to take the lead too. Pressure would really start to mount if that happened. Within five minutes we were able to heave a sigh of relief as fans with radios or mobiles confirmed that Orient had equalised against Oxford. As half-time approached and United began to get a slightly firmer grip on the game, another crucial scoreline came through: Notts County 0 Bury 1. Phew! If either of those scores remained the same Torquay could afford to lose and still stay up.

No changes at half-time, except that United began to look more confident and comfortable in the second half. Steven Reed warmed the goalie's hands with a rasping free kick, whilst the midfield took control to make sure that the defence was rarely troubled. Boston seemed to have accepted the draw, and looked content to wait for the final whistle and go home to pack for their well-deserved summer holiday. With no developments in the other key matches, the fans could start to relax a little and enjoy the last-day party atmosphere. Old boy Lee Canoville received a good natured chorus of boos when he limped from the field, then towards the end Jo Kuffour got a standing ovation as he made way for Tony Bedeau. Hollands, Bedeau and Thorpe went close but basically it was all about playing out time and waiting for the final final whistle of the season.

> A group of people have been waiting at a bus stop for over half an hour. Still no sign of a bus. To relieve the boredom a woman asks if anyone knows a good joke.
> **First Man**: I know a cracking Chelsea joke.
> **Second Man**: That's not fair, I'm a Chelsea fan!
> **First Man**: Don't worry mate, we'll explain it to you afterwards!

When that eventually came thousands of overjoyed fans, having listened politely to the numerous announcements that they must not under any circumstances run on the pitch.... ran on the pitch. Who'd be a steward, eh? One wild, screaming supporter invading the pitch you can deal with. Three or four maybe at a pinch. But four thousand???

When the crowd had had their frolic (and hopefully got into one of the Herald Express photos) the pitch was cleared and the exhausted but delighted players returned to take their bow and receive presentations. Kevin Hill scooped the awards for Overall Club Player of the Season and SMS Text Vote Player of the Season (well-deserved, though Andy Marriott must have come a very close second) and Tony Bedeau received the shield as Top Scorer.

Then, at last, we all went home for tea.

Joke!

> **Post-match Quotes:**
>
> *"What a horrible game that was!"*
> **Ian Atkins.**
>
> *"I don't think I've ever felt so nervous before a game."*
> **Darren Garner.**
>
> *"Everyone wrote us off a few weeks ago. The Gaffer has taken the pressure off everybody, and he deserves a hell of a lot of credit. Let's face it, he's kept us in the League."*
> **Player of the Year Kevin Hill.**

And so they all lived happily ever after .... or maybe not.

Of course the work didn't finish at 5 o'clock on Saturday 6th May. There were other matters that needed sorting out. Such as the minor issues of who would be managing the club next season, and which players would he have playing for him!

After the remarkable turnaround since Ian Atkins took over, it was inevitable that he would be asked to stay on next year. Chairman Mike Bateson wasted no time in making him an 'attractive' offer. After a few days to think things over he was unveiled as the manager who would lead United into the new season.

Meanwhile, it emerged that of the 28 players still on the books, only two, Martin Phillips and Matt Hewlett, had contracts for next season (almost all players are signed on one-year contracts before each season). Clearly there was a lot of talking, phoning and negotiating to be done in order to finalise a squad ready for pre-season training in July.

The majority of players, even at Division 2 level, have agents who will do all the dealing for them. That takes a weight off the player's shoulders, but also makes the whole business more time consuming. The chairman has to call the agent and make an offer, which the agent then takes to the player. The player will tell the agent what he thinks of the offer and then the agent gets back to the chairman to relay the news, etc etc etc. As you can imagine, this one can run and run. On top of all that the agent then takes his 10% of the money. During the Andy Marriott will-he-stay-or-will-he-go saga in June, thesituation was summed up Ian Atkins:

"The way things are going with agents in the game now, you can't believe anything till it actually happens. It's got to fever pitch. And the agents are not doing it for the good of the players, I can tell you that!"

Chairman Mike Bateson was even more blunt:

"Agents don't give a monkey's about things like the uprooting involved for families when a players moves. All they want is their commission cheque. It's surprising more players haven't seen through that."

He also highlighted a further problem resulting from each player having a different agent doing the deals for him:

"If you end up with players of the same ability but very different wages in the dressing room, that's a recipe for problems."

Just imagine how you would feel if you were as old as another player in the team, had been at the club just as long, were working just as hard as him and playing just as well, but he was earning a lot more than you because his agent had managed to get a better deal from the club than yours! Surely it would be much better (and faster) if the deals were done purely between the player and the club, with no middle-man?

While all this is going on the manager has to look around for new players. He would have told the chairman at the end of the season which players he wanted to keep, and so he'd now be phoning round to try to get players to fill the gaps that were left. He'd also be unsure of which of his squad were going to accept the contracts they'd been offered for the next season. The whole midfield might be weighing up their options about staying or going. It would be no use sitting back expecting all of them to sign on the dotted line. What if two of them decided to move on to another club? What if all four of them did??? You'd look a right Charlie turning up for pre-season training with no midfield players! The phone would need to be red hot and the phone bill even more frightening than most of your mobile bills! (n dnt try n tel me u hardly eva use yr fone, cos Torbay Hospital iz ful ov crazy jabberin prnts who cower n cringe in dark cornaz weneva dey c an nvelope wiv Orange/T-Mobile/ Vodafone on it). N if u can read all dat, u obviously r a serious txtr, so quit tryin 2 fool me m8!

As the dust settled after the Boston game it was revealed that Connell, Robinson, Sako and Priso would have to look for other clubs. James Sharp was also on his way - a shame after his great service as player and captain during the injury-hit mid-season. Lloyd, Afful and Clay Bond were given the option of proving themselves when training started again in July.

By the Thursday Hill, Hockley, Taylor, Thorpe and Villis had all put pen to paper on new contracts. After that it was a waiting game, as Marriott, Garner, Bedeau, Kuffour and Hollands all went away to think over the offers they'd received. The situation was further complicated by the fact that the loan players had to find out whether their own clubs wanted to keep them or not before they could make a decision about staying at Torquay.

A couple of days later came the welcome news that Woodsy had agreed terms and would be back next year. The following week Mickey Evans was signed from Plymouth to strengthen the attack. Which

> **Surely they didn't really say that???**
>
> "I'd like to play for an Italian club, like Barcelona."
>
> "Germany are a very difficult team to play...they had 11 internationals out there today."
>
> "I couldn't settle in Italy - it was like living in a foreign country."
>
> "I wouldn't be bothered if we lost every game as long as we won the league."
>
> "I've never wanted to leave. I'm here for the rest of my life, and hopefully after that as well."
>
> "I'm as happy as I can be - but I have been happier."
>
> "I can see the carrot at the end of the tunnel."
>
> "I always used to put my right boot on first, and then obviously my right sock."
>
> Turn to page 159 to find out which ones are true!

turned out just as well really, as a short while later the chairman received a 12-word text from Tony Bedeau's agent to say that he was signing for another club. Charming! (What's the shortest text he could have sent - 'TB off. Soz' maybe?) Tony later phoned to apologise for his agent's actions, and he will no doubt be given a warm reception when Warsaw next visit Plainmoor.

As the Football League play-offs came to an end we were dealt one last financial blow when Swansea narrowly missed out on promotion to the Championship, going down on penalties to Barnsley in the play-offs. In a typically complicated deal United would have picked up a further £25,000 on the transfer of Akinfenwa if Swansea had gone up. Ironically it was Torquay local lad Danny Nardiello who scored the equaliser for Barnsley to take the game into extra time!

June brought both good and bad news. First the good: we heard that Leroy was returning to full management at Brentford - I'm sure they'll benefit from his tactical flair. Now the bad : Andy Marriott's contract negotiations took one final twist. Having made a verbal agreement to stay, we then found out that he'd signed for Boston. A sad farewell to the club for the man who'd done more than anyone to keep us in the league with his brilliant displays all the way through last season. And as if that wasn't enough Jo Kuffour, who seemed to have agreed to a new one-year contract to stay at Plainmoor, then announced that he was moving to Brentford instead. Ho hum.

I suppose you could argue that Marriott was getting close to the end of his career, and new young blood was needed. However, goalies tend to get better with age, often playing their best football in their thirties, and it would be hard to replace Andy's consistency. It would also have been nice to bring in another promising youngster who might learn from Marriott and be ready to take over next season.

Similarly you might say that Kuffour's performances had been rather hit and miss last season, so it was no great loss if he left. But for an attack to be really dangerous it needs some pace, and Jo had plenty of that. With him lurking about, ready to seize on any mistake, defences would be nervous about pushing forward. His goals in those last crucial games had shown what an asset he could be to the club - he just needed a manager who could get those displays from him week in week out instead of every so often.

By the end of June Darren Garner had agreed to a new deal, and both Steven Reed and Lee Andrews could now officially become Torquay players as their contracts ended at Yeovil and Carlisle. As pre-season training started again in early July the squad was still looking very thin though, and the fans were beginning to get very restless. Their fears were calmed with two exciting signings in the space of a few days. First Lee Mansell, a battling midfielder, joined the club from Oxford, then Jamie Ward, a youngster on Aston Villa's books, arrived to fill Jo Kuffour's boots on the wing. Ok, so we still didn't have a goaly, but surely that minor problem could be overcome before the start of the new season.... maybe we could play without one, setting a new trend in ultra-attacking tactics - a 0-4-4-3 system which would pen the opposition back in their own half so effectively that they'd be limited to taking 60-yard potshots. We'd win every game 8-7 or 12-10 without a goaly, the crowds would come flooding back, United would gain promotion by a record margin, build a fantastic new state-of-the-art stadium, have the top names in world football fighting to sign on even if it meant a cut in salary, after three successive promotions we'd win the Premiership, FA Cup and Champions League treble, England would win the next World Cup with a squad containing 12 Torquay players, Craig Taylor would be crowned king..................

Blimey that was scary! I just woke up from this totally weird nightmare that I'd written a book about Torquay United! Thank God it was just a dream, I can't stand writers - lazy good-for-nothing wasters who sit on their bums all day drinking coffee, dozing and daydreaming..........

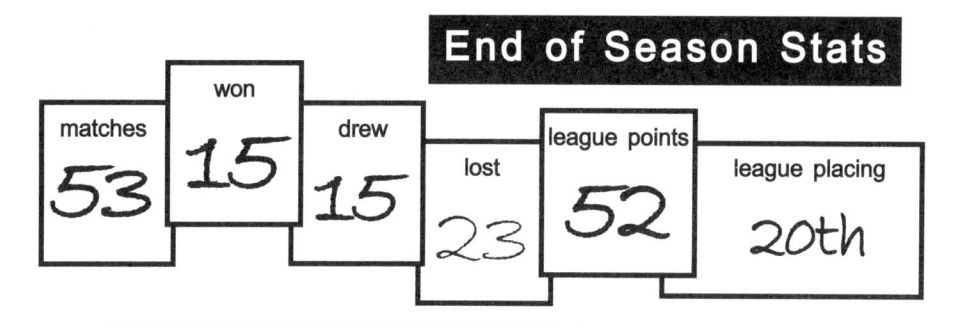

End of Season Stats

- matches: **53**
- won: **15**
- drew: **15**
- lost: **23**
- league points: **52**
- league placing: **20th**

- goals scored: **57**
- scorers: see chart on page 153
- goals conceded: **73**

- players used: **33**
- average match time in possession of ball: **47%**
- yellow cards: **63**
- red cards: **6**

- fouls by United: **596**
- fouls by opponents: **741**
- goal attempts by United: **535**
- goal attempts by opponents: **630**

- total attendance: **202,328** (Ave: 3,818)
- total miles travelled: **12,912**

Table at end of season

	P	W	D	L	F	A	GD	Pts
Carlisle Utd	46	25	11	10	84	42	42	86
Northampton	46	22	17	7	63	37	26	83
Leyton Orient	46	22	15	9	67	51	16	81
Grimsby Town	46	22	12	12	64	44	20	78
Cheltenham	46	19	15	12	65	53	12	72
Wycombe W.	46	18	17	11	72	56	16	71
Lincoln City	46	15	21	10	65	53	12	66
Darlington	46	16	15	15	58	52	6	63
Peterborough	46	17	11	18	57	49	8	62
Shrewsbury	46	16	13	17	55	55	0	61
Boston United	46	15	16	15	50	60	-10	61
Bristol Rovers	46	17	9	20	59	67	-8	60
Wrexham	46	15	14	17	61	54	7	59
Rochdale	46	14	14	18	66	69	-3	56
Chester City	46	14	12	20	53	59	-6	54
Mansfield T.	46	13	15	18	59	66	-7	54
Macclesfield	46	12	18	16	60	71	-11	54
Barnet	46	12	18	16	44	57	-13	54
Bury	46	12	17	17	45	57	-12	53
Torquay Utd	**46**	**13**	**13**	**20**	**53**	**66**	**-13**	**52**
Notts County	46	12	16	18	48	63	-15	52
Stockport C.	46	11	19	16	57	78	-21	52
Oxford United	46	11	16	19	43	57	-14	49
Rushden/D.	46	11	12	23	44	76	-32	45

May

ALPHABET QUIZ

A home of Liverpool FC

N recent England international brothers

B Michael, Chelsea's German skipper

O Martin, new Aston Villa manager

C brothers in 1966 World Cup team

P Premiership club playing at Fratton Park

D Jermain, Spurs striker

Q Frank, Middlesborough defender

E this stadium is Arsenal's new home

R Raith, Doncaster or Blackburn?

F manager and knight (that's Sir to you!)

S Premiership's all-time top scorer

G Man United's Welsh wizard winger

T Everton's tasty nickname!

H these two clubs are Edinburgh rivals

U this Park is home to West Ham ....

I Championship team, FA Cup winners 1978

V .... and this Road is where Watford play

J England goalie, frequent visitor to Shaldon

W youngest of England's 2006 squad

K Robbie, Spurs Irish striker

X Alonso, Liverpool midfielder

L Chelsea and England midfield star

Y our Somerset Div 1 neighbours

M is this manager really The Special One?

Z Bobby, West Ham striker

Score Ratings:

22 - 26	True Football Fan	16 - 21	Keen Amateur Fan
10 - 15	Armchair Fan	0 - 9	Chelsea Fan???

Answers p 159

Extras

The Players Speak!

Ever thought that football has some silly rules? If the FA gave you the power to change one thing about the game, what would you do? Here are some of the viewpoints of the Torquay players and coaches:

- Send a player off if he's caught diving. It's cheating and we need it out of the game.

- Stop giving goalies so much protection when they jump for a ball. When a centre-half and a striker challenge for the same ball it's a real 50/50 contest. When a goaly goes up with a striker it seems that any contact with the goaly results in a free-kick. Not fair on the attacking team.

- Get rid of the new offside rule and go back to the old one. The change to the rule introduced a couple of years ago says that a player is only given offside if the ref decides that he is in an 'active' position. In other words, if he's standing in an offside position but nowhere near the play, or is running back towards his own goal, he's not considered to be active, and the ref waves play on. As more than one coach has said: "If he's not active he's not doing his job and so shouldn't be on the pitch in the first place!" Many top people in the game believe that this rule makes the ref's job impossible, and would prefer the old system: if there aren't at least two opponents between you and their goal, you're offside. Full stop!

- Stop booking players after goal celebrations. What's wrong with someone showing their emotions at such a fantastic moment???

- Bring in video technology to judge on issues such as whether a ball has crossed the goal line or not. With so much money at stake these days, why not use technology to make sure we get those crucial decisions right every time?

- Introduce the rugby 'sin-bin' system into football too. If a player argues with the ref, kicks the ball away after a decision or stands in the way of a free kick to stop the opposition taking it quickly, he could be sent to the sin-bin for ten minutes. Booking the player doesn't really give the opposition an advantage, but playing against ten men for ten minutes certainly would. Maybe then they'd stop being so annoying!

Ever wanted to be a professional footballer? We asked the squad for viewpoints on the best and worst things about the job:

First the best bits:

- Short working hours and lots of free time!
- Feeling fit, strong and healthy.
- The excitement of playing in important matches in front of big crowds.
- The money!
- Doing a job I've always wanted to do, and which I love doing, and getting well paid for it too.

And now the worst bits:

- Long away trips - all the travelling and sitting around in hotels.
- Having to get another job when I retire.
- Stress (it's not always an easy life!)
- Being stereotyped (everybody thinks footballers are a bit thick!)
- Working over Christmas. (Especially true for players with kids)
- Everybody thinks you're rich.
- Losing!

Want to know what to do if you still want to be a footballer? We asked the players what advice they would give to a hopeful teenager:

- Work hard and never give up trying.
- Give it 100% in both training and matches, and stay out of trouble!
- Keep up with your studies - if you don't make it as a player you'll need other skills to fall back on.
- Be dedicated. Don't let other distractions get in your way.
- Be prepared to be a good loser. You can't win all the time, and when you lose don't take it out on friends and family!
- Take in as much advice as you can, especially from people who have a lot of experience in the game.

So there you have it! The recipe for success, from the people who've been there, done that, bought the T-shirt and licked the lolly! *(what???)*

And now, to finish off, just a few more stats ....

Goal Distribution

Opposition		Gulls
②①	0-5	①②③
③②①	6-10	①②③④⑤
⑦⑥⑤④③②①	11-15	①②
⑥⑤④③②①	16-20	①②
②①	21-25	①②③④
②①	26-30	①②③
	31-35	①②
①	36-40	①
⑤④③②①	41-45	①②③④⑤
⑥⑤④③②①	46-50	①②
③②①	51-55	①②③④
④③②①	56-60	①②
④③②①	61-65	①②③④
⑦⑥⑤④③②①	66-70	①②③④⑤⑥
②①	71-75	①
⑤④③②①	76-80	①②
⑦⑥⑤④③②①	81-85	①
⑦⑥⑤④③②①	86-90	①②③④⑤⑥⑦⑧

This table shows when the goals were scored, both for and against, in United's matches. The 90 minutes is broken into 5-minute sections.

What can we learn from this table? Maybe ....

● United were quick out of the blocks - they outscored their opponents in the first 10 minutes of matches.

● After soaking up early pressure, oppositions then hit back well, as they scored United 13-4 between the 10th and 20th minutes.

● The period from the 25th to 40th minute tended to be a quiet spell in most games, but the last few minutes of the half saw an increase in scoring (but these periods at the end of each half do include time added on).

● United appear to have started the second half slowly, scoring only twice in the first 5 minutes. Not fully focussed after the half-time break?

● Although they scored their fair share of late goals, the ten minute period between the 75th and 85th minute was a disaster zone - 12 goals conceded to only 3 scored. Maybe a lack of concentration? Tiredness?

Player	Starts	Apps as sub	Goals	Discipline	Gulls Mad Ave Score *
ANDREWS, Lee	6	1	0		6.1
BEDEAU, Tony	35	5	11	[2] [1]	5.9
COLEMAN, Liam	9	9	0	[2]	6.5
CONNELL, Alan	13	11	7	[1]	6.6
CONSTANTINE, Leon	11	6	1	[3]	5.8
GARNER, Darren	44	3	2	[11]	6.4
HEWLETT, Matt	21	7	1	[5]	5.8
HILL, Kevin	47	2	9	[5]	6.1
HOCKLEY, Matt	30	10	0	[5]	6.1
HOLLANDS, Danny	10	0	1	[1]	6.5
KUFFOUR, Jo	39	10	9	[1]	6.5
LAWLESS, Alex	13	3	0		6.3
LLOYD, Anthony	23	2	0	[1]	6.5
LOCKWOOD, Adam	12	0	3	[1]	6.9
MARRIOTT, Andy	53	0	0		7.2
McGLINCHEY, Brian	4	1	0		6.7
PHILLIPS, Martin	27	4	3	[1]	6.7
REED, Steven	11	0	0		6.4
ROBINSON, Paul	12	9	3	[1]	6.4
SAKO, Morike	13	14	3	[3] [1]	6.5
SHARP, James	37	2	0	[7]	6.8
SOW, Mamadou	9	7	0	[1]	5.9
STONEBRIDGE, Ian	5	0	1	[1]	7.0
TAYLOR, Craig	35	5	0	[3] [1]	6.7
THORPE, Lee	10	0	3	[2] [1]	6.7
VILLIS, Matt	13	1	0	[2]	6.5
WOODS, Steve	40	4	0	[6]	6.3

Also played: AFFUL Les (0,5,0,1Y); FLYNN Patrick (1,0,0,0Y); HANCOX Richard (0,1,0,0Y); McALISKEY John (3,0,0,0Y); PRISO Carl (1,1,0,1Y); WOODMAN Craig (4,0,0,1Y);

*Players are given a score out of 10 for each game. For more info, try visiting Gulls Mad at www.torquayunited-mad.co.uk

Last stats before bedtime .....

- Of the 19 games when United scored first, they won 12 and only lost 4. In the 22 games when their opponents scored first, however, United only picked up 8 points (1 win and 5 draws), the worst in the division.

- United's average score was 1.15 - 1.43. In other words, they scored an average of just over one goal per game, but their opponents scored nearly one and a half goals per game.

- United kept 14 clean sheets during the season. Of those games they won 9 and drew 5. Andy Marriott played every minute of every game.

- They performed better against the teams in the top half of the table (9 wins from 24 games). Of their 22 games against lower table opponents they won only 4 (the worst record in the division). This suggests maybe that they rose to the challenge of playing teams at or near the top.

- United's record of converting half-time leads into victories was the worst in Division 2. They were up in 11 games at half-time, but only managed to hang on to that lead in 5 matches. Could that be down to fitness, concentration or confidence? They did better when only drawing at half-time, losing only 5 of those 19 games - the 6th best record in the division.

- The British record for boring people with stats is held by a Mr Adrian Bradbury of Torquay, who took only 34.72 minutes to put 185 children to sleep by forcing them to read the stats section of his book about Torquay United. He received a cheque for £19.95 from his sponsors Nytol, which he put towards a new anorak with matching notebook and mittens.

Answers

p 9   Torquay Till I Die: 1. Plainmoor; 2. b) 6000; 3. £5; 4. Yellow and Blue; 5. Leroy Rosenior, John Cornforth, Ian Atkins; 6. Frank Prince; 7. Boston United; 8. The Gulls; 9. Gilbert The Gull; 10. a) Craig; b) Stevland; c) Darren; d) Lee.

p 25   Can You Believe That!!! Are you serious??? It was pure nonsense from the first word to the last. Derr!!!

p27

	P	W	D	L	F	A	GD	Pts
T.U.F.C.	15	8	3	4	33	18	15	28

p 28   Total penalties: 170 (34 x 5) + 8 = <u>178</u>   Faced by each goaly: divide by 2 = <u>89</u>

7:45 + 3 + 45 + 2 + 15 + 45 + 4 = <u>9:39pm</u>, which on a 24-hour clock is <u>21:39</u>

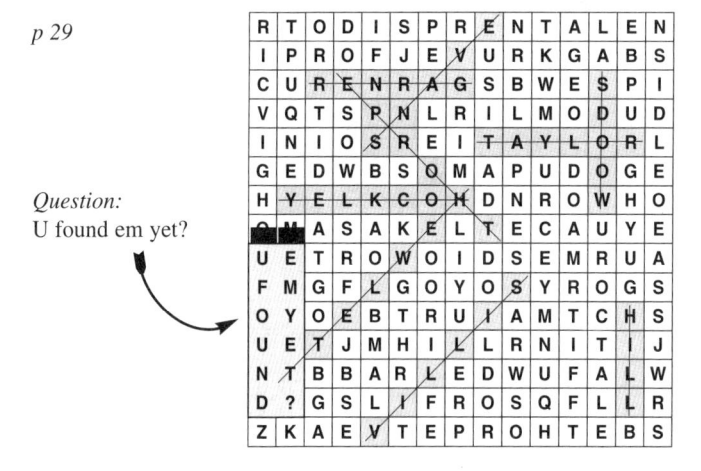

p 29

Question:
U found em yet?

p 31   Penalty Area = 35 x 15 = <u>525m²</u>   Pitch = 100 x 55 = <u>5500m²</u>
Shuttle Run = 100 + 150 + 300 + 400 = <u>950m</u>

p 32   Twenty coachloads of Gulls fans made the long trip down to Barcelona for the club's first ever European match last night. The home team were so ***confident*** that they decided to leave superstar Ronaldinho on the bench, whilst Torquay put out a strong defensive team, playing a 4-5-1 ***formation*** with Thorpe on his own up front.

United were put under ***pressure*** from the off, and went a goal behind when Etoo got the better of Woods in the air to send a header ***looping*** over everyone and in off the far post. Things went from bad to worse when Garner had to leave the field with a calf injury just before half-time.

The second half followed a ***similar*** pattern to the first, with United on the back foot for long spells. Needing a second goal Barcelona sent on Ronaldinho after an hour, and ***despite*** heroic defence United went two down ten minutes from time. A mazy dribble by that man Ronaldinho ended when he was brought down by a ***desperate*** Hockley tackle. The Brazilian took the spot kick himself and coolly slotted the ball into the bottom corner, sending the keeper the ***wrong*** way.

With the game nearing the end Torquay needed a miracle, and it arrived when a defensive mix-up let in Thorpe. He used his strength to break free and then ***lobbed*** the ball over the stranded keeper to give United a vital away goal.

The return leg at Plainmoor is already sold out, though the whole match will be shown live on a ***giant*** screen in Castle Circus. Get there early!

p 33   Woods: 250 x 4 = <u>1000kg</u>;   Hill: 300 x 5 = <u>1500kg</u>;   Hockley: <u>450 sit-ups</u>

p 40   Who Am I? (1) Matt Hockley; Craig Taylor; Matt Villis.

p 53

P	R	O	T	E	I	N		F
L		P		N				R
A	L	E	X		D	I	V	E
I		R		O				E
N	E	A	R	P	O	S	T	
M		T		R			O	G
O	N	I	O	N	S		W	
O		O					N	
R	A	N	G	E	R	S		

p 54   There are 6 combinations: TW; TP; TH; WP; WH; PH.

With Evans, now 10 possibilities: TW; TP; TH; TE; WP; WH; WE; PH; PE; HE.

p 55   The 11 mistakes, followed by the correct spellings, are: desided/<u>decided</u>; forth/<u>fourth</u>; ratteled/<u>rattled</u>; war/<u>wore</u>; visiters/<u>visitors</u>; exllent/<u>excellent</u>; suprise/<u>surprise</u>; poor/<u>pour</u>; bought/<u>brought</u>; unstopable/<u>unstoppable</u>; privent/<u>prevent</u>.

p 56   scarf, burger, chips, programme;   referee, crossbar, corner flag;

Nottingham (Notts County!), Darlington, Rochdale, Mansfield, Peterborough, Barnet.

p 57   There are 26 rectangles altogether in the picture. (Trust me!)

p 58

	P	W	D	L	F	A	GD	Pts
Aston Villa	30	14	**14**	2	57	34	23	56
Reading	**30**	15	7	8	49	32	17	**52**
Torquay Utd	30	15	6	9	51	29	**22**	51
Man Utd	30	**12**	14	4	55	27	28	50
Everton	29	12	11	6	48	36	12	**47**
Arsenal	29	11	10	8	42	**28**	14	43
Newcastle Utd	29	11	9	9	**41**	29	12	42
West Ham Utd	30	10	**10**	10	42	33	**9**	40

p 64   Who Am I? (2)   Kevin Hill;   Darren Garner;   Matt Hewlett.

p 88   1 = cranium;   2 = collar bone;   3 = ribs;   4 = hamstring;   5 = femur;   6 = tibia
7 = achilles tendon;   8 = metatarsals;   9 = calf;   10 = fibula;   11 = patella;
12 = quadriceps;   13 = pelvis;   14 = vertebra

p 89   Beckham: £1.75m or £1,750,000;   Ronaldo: £0.6m or £600,000;
Villis: £20,000;   Lampard: £1.6m or £1,600,000;   Shufflebottom: £400;
Ronaldinho: £2.85m, or £2,850,000.

p 91   Billy: Mushy peas (70p) + tea (65p) = £1.35, £1.50 left for a <u>Steak Pasty</u>.
Bobby: Pizza (90p) + two crisps (90p) + Bovril (60p) = <u>£2.40</u>.
Berty: Chicken pie and chips = £1.95, taken away from £2.80 is 85p - <u>a coffee</u>.
Barry: £2.40 - Bovril (60p) = £1.80. He could've had <u>two pizza slices</u> or <u>a curry pasty and crisps</u>.
Betty: Beef pie (£1.20), two hot dogs (£2.50), burger (£1.30), two chips (£1.60), tea (65p), and three soft drinks (£1.65) comes to £8.90 altogether.
That leaves £3.15, which at 45p a packet makes <u>7 packets of crisps</u>.

p 92   *ubiquitous* means everywhere or involved in everything, which is a good thing!
flamboyant means exciting/dazzling (good);   *execrable* means awful!
dynamic means energetic (good);   *ingenious* means crafty/skilful (good);
diffident means hesitant/timid (bad);   *indefatigable* means tireless (good).

If there was no time added on, a match starting at 7:30 would finish at 9:15. Our additions here are 6 + 5 + 30 + 2 + 8 + 13 = 64 minues, which means that the game would finally finish at <u>10:19</u>. On a 24-hour clock this would be <u>22:19</u>.

p 93   A = Harlepool Utd;   B = Lincoln City;   C = Wycombe Wanderers;   D = Torquay!!!
E = Bristol Rovers;   F = Walsall;   G = Shrewsbury Town;   H = Chester City;
I = Stockport County;   J = Accrington Stanley.

p 94   Lee: 270kg (45 x 6) + 225kg (45 x 5) + 180kg (45 x 4) = 675kg

Mickey: 8 + 7 + 6 = 21 reps. Multiplied by 35kg makes 735kg.
So <u>Mickey lifted 60kg more than Lee.</u>

Matt V did 44 reps altogether. If you divide that into the total weight lifted (660kg) the answer is <u>15kg</u>.

Matt H gained 1.65 kg (76.25 - 74.60). As there are 1000g in 1kg, that's <u>1650g</u>.

p 104   Nicknames: Mansfield - Stags; Walsall - Saddlers; Macclesfield - Silkmen; Notts County - Magpies; Boston - Pilgrims; Bury - Shakers; Barnet - Bees; Chester - Exiles; Darlington - Quakers.

Grounds: Memorial Stadium - Bristol Rovers; Edgeley Park - Stockport County; Nene Park - Rushden and Diamonds; Gay Meadow - Shrewsbury Town; Racecourse Ground - Wrexham; Spotland - Rochdale.

p 118   Now You're The Ref! 1. <u>Goal</u>! An indirect free-kick has to be touched by someone for a goal to be awarded. All a player's kit is judged to be part of his body, so flicking a shirt counts as being touched.

2. No goal! Buster needs to get the ref's permission before he can come back onto the field. <u>Free kick for the opposition</u> and a yellow card for Hill.

3. You might think this would count as a foul throw, resulting in a throw to the opposition, but the correct way of restarting the game is with a <u>goal kick</u>.

4. <u>Goal</u>! If the ball had been passed to Mickey by a team mate he would've been offside, but you can't be offside direct from a goal kick!

p 131   9 squared = 81. Multiply that by 3.14 = <u>254.34m^2</u>.

3.14 x 18 (diameter) = <u>56.52m</u>.

Can You Believe That!!! (2) Yes you can! (apart from the bath and baked beans!)

p 132 $105^2 + 65^2$ = 11025 + 4225 = 15250m. The square root of 15250, when rounded to 3 decimal places, is <u>123.491</u>. Rounded to 1 decimal place that becomes <u>123.5</u>.

p 133

	P	W	D	L	F	A	GD	Pts
Torquay Utd	38	28	7	3	97	45	52	91
Man Utd	38	22	7	9	73	43	30	73
West Ham Utd	38	21	6	11	58	43	15	69
Spurs	38	19	10	9	51	30	21	67
Aston Villa	38	18	11	9	53	34	19	65
Liverpool	38	15	13	10	46	35	11	58
Watford	38	16	10	12	57	56	1	58
Middlesborough	38	16	7	15	55	55	0	55
Macclesfield	38	15	10	13	52	53	-1	55
Bolton Wanderers	38	15	8	15	57	49	8	53
Blackburn Rovers	38	14	10	14	63	54	9	52
Leeds Utd	38	14	10	14	46	52	-6	52

p 134   There are <u>15</u> possible back 4s : AHTR; AHTW; AHTV; AHRW; AHRV; AHWV; ATRW; ATRV; ATWV; ARWV; HTRW; HTRV; HTWV; HRWV; TRWV.

ANDREWS = 84; HOCKLEY = 79; TAYLOR = 91; REED = 32; WOODS = 76; VILLIS = 83. So if you take out the two lowest totals, the highest combination would be <u>Hockley, Villis, Andrews and Taylor (total 337)</u>.

p 135   Marriott easily plucked the cross out of the air.
Sharp caused problems with his long throws into the area.
The Gulls started the second half as they had finished the first.
United held out to clinch three vital points.
The Gulls got off to a flying start thanks to Jo Kuffour's second minute belter.
Phillips gave the goalie no chance with an angled shot into the bottom corner.

p 137

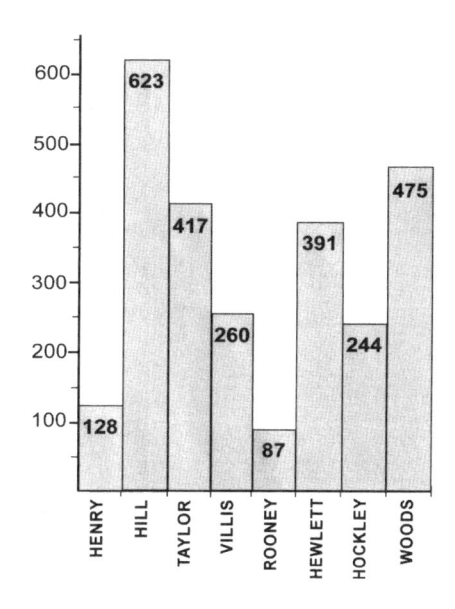

Bar chart values: HENRY = 128; HILL = 623; TAYLOR = 417; VILLIS = 260; ROONEY = 87; HEWLETT = 391; HOCKLEY = 244; WOODS = 475.

p144   Surely they didn't really say that??? 'Fraid so! All actual quotes by top footballers!

p148   Alphabet Quiz: Anfield; Ballack; Charlton; Defoe; Emirates; Ferguson; Giggs; Hearts/Hibs; Ipswich; James; Keane; Lampard; Mourinho; Neville; O'Neill; Portsmouth; Queudrue; Rovers; Shearer; Toffees; Upton; Vicarage; Walcott; Xabi; Yeovil; Zamora.

Photo Quizzes:
Sack The Photographer! A - Kevin Hill; B - Craig Taylor; C - Steven Reed; D - Darren Garner; E - Matt Villis; F - Lee Thorpe; G - Martin Phillips; H - Steve Woods.

Test Your Memory! 1. Leon Constantine; 2. Jo Kuffour; 3. Danny Hollands; 4. Paul Robinson; 5. Anthony Lloyd; 6. Liam Coleman; 7. Alan Connell; 8. Brian McGlinchey; 9. Ian Stonebridge; 10. Adam Lockwood; 11. James Sharp; 12. Tony Bedeau; 13. Morike Sako; 14. Alex Lawless; 15. Andy Marriott.

Strip!   A - 1992; B - 1996; C - 1935; D - 2004; E - 1957; F - 1975.

CONGRATULATIONS!

You've reached the end! I bet you thought you'd never make it. You haven't skipped bits, have you? I really hope not, because then I'd have to find out where you live and come and get you, which would be a real pain as I'm a very busy man. Books don't just write themselves you know! There's tea and coffee to be drunk (which of course means I have to pop out to the shop for bikkies now and then), endless hours of daydreaming to be done, at least three sessions a day of staring vacantly out of a window, not to mention regular trips to Plainmoor to watch United ~~get hamm~~ clinch yet another famous victory.

Well, I hope you've enjoyed it all. If you'd like to tell me which bits you liked best, or have any useful comments to make, please feel free to get in touch with me at:

bobby_dazzler@fsmail.net

I *will* reply, I promise! On the other hand, if you have any criticisms or negative feedback, you can contact me via my alternative E-mail address:

getlost@fsmail.nuts

See ya!

AB.